T0244169

One Month in
Sonoma Wine Country

AN EXPERT'S GUIDE:
"Top 30 Wineries and Top 30 Restaurants in Sonoma County"

RONNIE COLEMAN

One Month in Sonoma Wine Country

An Expert's Guide: "Top 30 Wineries and Top 30 Restaurants in Sonoma County

© 2023, Ronnie Coleman.

Print ISBN: 979-8-35092-907-2

eBook ISBN: 979-8-35092-908-9

DISCLAIMER

All content, narrative, and opinions presented in this book are based on my personal experiences, observations, and interactions at the described wineries and restaurants in Sonoma Wine Country. Any information included is either derived from direct encounters at these establishments, gleaned from publicly accessible sources, or shared during casual interactions.

While I have made every effort to portray each establishment with honesty and integrity, this book does not purport to provide an exhaustive or definitive representation of any winery, restaurant, organization, individual or group. It is a reflection of my personal journey and perspective. The views and opinions expressed herein are solely my own and do not reflect or represent those of any entity or individual mentioned.

All photographs in this book were taken by me or my traveling companion with a small handheld camera. To respect privacy, all recognizable faces, including those of individuals in the background, have been blurred or otherwise obscured.

Readers are advised that this book is intended as a personal narrative and guide. Relying on its content is at one's discretion. Neither I nor my publisher will be responsible or liable for any misunderstandings, misinterpretations or any issues arising from the content within.

ACKNOWLEDGEMENT

I want to give special thanks to Rusty Gaffney, the famed "Prince of Pinot". After retiring from his ophthalmology practice in 2001, Rusty began writing an online newsletter, "The PinotFile", which was the first wine publication devoted to pinot noir.

I liked pinot noir before I began reading The PinotFile a couple of decades ago, but it wasn't long before Rusty's enthusiasm, insight, and recommendations had me loving pinot noir.

It wasn't just the wine recommendations (and later the scores) that intrigued me about Rusty's writing. He almost always told the story of the people behind the wine such that you felt like you knew them better after reading each issue of the PinotFile.

It was that approach of telling the story of the people behind the label that I have somewhat emulated in this book. I am always intrigued by the backstories of the winery owners, the winemakers, the vineyard managers, etc. The same holds true for restaurants, as you will see in this book.

Rusty gave me tremendous joy over the couple of decades or so that he wrote the newsletter. I felt a void when he recently retired from writing the PinotFile. However, the newsletter still has more great information about (mainly domestic) pinot noir (and occasionally other varietals) than one might find pretty much anywhere.

When I traveled to a wine destination over the years (places like Oregon, Santa Cruz Mountains, Santa Barbara County, Napa and yes—Sonoma), Rusty would make recommendations for not only wineries but also for restaurants and more.

His suggestions were always spot on, and I have had great times over the years based on his insights. This gentleman knows more about pinot noir, the vineyards, how it is produced, and the people behind the wineries than I could remotely ever hope to know.

I appreciate his knowledge, his writing skills and for always taking the time to suggest venues to me over the years. Cheers Rusty!

CONTENTS

Imagine savoring the beauty of Sonoma Wine Country not just for a quick weekend or hurried week but instead spending an entire month amongst the wineries and the restaurants that abound throughout the County. Introducing: One Month in Sonoma Wine Country.

Starting many years back, each visit for me was like a race against time—an intense attempt to experience all the exceptional wineries (over 400) and as many restaurants as possible in an abbreviated period. After these shorter trips, I was exhausted, with a blurry head full of beautiful memories and a few extra pounds to match.

Recognizing this, I dreamed up a more balanced approach: One Month in Wine Country—which I executed for the last five years! The plan was beautifully simple: visit one winery and one restaurant per day, with mornings dedicated to a vigorous gym session.

Though it looked simple on paper to execute, this 30-day indulgence proved way more challenging than anticipated. Drinking consecutively for 30 days, whether at restaurants, wineries, or both, will (and did) take a toll—but I survived to chronicle it all!

Therefore, you will notice some repetitive words or phrases in this book, like "buzzed," "hungover", "stumbled in," "French fries," and more. Speaking of repetition, you'll also observe that Duck and Pinot Noir is something that I order a whole lot.

For those who can't spare a whole month, fear not. This book allows you to explore Sonoma at your own pace, offering a curated list of My Top 30 Wineries and My Top 30 Restaurants in Sonoma Wine Country (plus, at the end of the book, a special section with my "Top 3 Lists" and my "Top Winery" and "Top Restaurant" in Sonoma).

I was fortunate enough to have my talented photographer, Colleen, accompany me on this vibrant adventure, capturing the essence of the best wineries and the most delightful restaurants Sonoma offers. She also sometimes imbibed with me, which might explain quite a few blurry pictures. But we weren't going for perfection; we were going for great experiences—and we were successful!

This journey is more than just a tour of tastings; it's an invitation into the heart of Sonoma. We'll wander through Farmer's Markets, meet passionate Olive Oil Producers and cheese artisans, and discover the perfect spots for a picturesque picnic.

At the core of this book and this experience are the stories of the remarkable people who shape (and have shaped) Sonoma's character—the passionate owners, visionary founders, and dedicated staff of the wineries and restaurants we will visit.

So, come with us. We're thrilled to have you join this lively, unvarnished and heartfelt expedition through Sonoma's stunning landscapes, rich flavors, and, most importantly, its vibrant community of people and their stories.

I've organized the book into sections by partitioning the County and its corresponding cities, making it easier to explore specific parts of the County. Welcome to One Month in Sonoma Wine Country!

HEALDSBURG/
NORTH COUNTY

TOWNS:

HEALDSBURG & GEYSERVILLE

MCROSTIE WINERY ESTATE HOUSE

There is nothing more welcoming in Wine Country than having a member of the winery staff walk towards you with glasses of wine, greeting you well before you get to the check-in area. Welcome to McRostie Estate Wine House on the world-famous Westside Road in Healdsburg, where that greeting made us feel special right away.

Starting in 1974 (when there were about 40 wineries in Sonoma), Steve McRostie began working at (the now-defunct) Hacienda Winery in Sonoma. McRostie established McRostie Winery in 1987 with a focus on Sonoma Coast chardonnay and pinot noir.

Aside from sourcing fruit from his vineyards, including the 14-acre pinot noir Thale Vineyard (Thale being his wife's name), which surrounds the winery, McRostie sources from about 30 additional chardonnay vineyards and around 15 pinot noir vineyards.

Heidi Bridenhagen was named just the third winemaker in McRostie history in 2013. Heidi was McRostie's assistant winemaker for two years (before that, Oyster Bay in New Zealand, Jackson Family, Clos

du Bois, and Sonoma-Cutrer), and, working along with Steve, has been instrumental in continuing to lift McRostie's stature.

With all the bottlings available at the winery, it's hard to pick a favorite. McRostie has forged relationships with some of the most respected vineyards in Sonoma County (such as Dutton, Martinelli, Bacigalupi, Sangiacamo, etc.).

Look for any varietal originating from Wildcat Mountain Vineyard (owned by McRostie and located in a mountainous, cool, windy, and foggy setting with volcanic soils). For pinot noir—Gap's Crown and Nightwing Vineyard. For chardonnay—Durrell Vineyard and Bacigalupi.

The winery visit offers a beautiful setting above Westside Road and has both inside and outside seating. We were outside on a beautiful fall day. We met a newly engaged couple from Scottsdale, Arizona, visiting with friends from Austin, Texas and Sandestin, Florida, who invited us to join their table for some Wildcat Mountain Chardonnay.

Every seat inside and out overlooks the estate vineyard, vineyards on the other side of Westside Road, and the mountains in the distance—the wine is delicious, and the setting is intimate, comfortable, and hard to beat in Sonoma Wine Country.

4605 Westside Road, Healdsburg .... 707-473-9303 .... www.macrostiewinery.com

ARISTA WINERY

Arista Winery was founded by Texas natives Janis and Al McWilliams in 2002. They purchased 36 acres on Silk Stocking Avenue for Pinot Noir (Westside Road) in 2004, and that is where the winery is located today (only about a half mile from the very well-known Williams Selyem).

Al and Janis turned the reins over to their two sons, Mark and Ben, in 2012, and they now run the day-to-day operations of the business. The wines are excellent!

I've interacted with Mark on several occasions, and he is very knowledgeable and has an engaging personality. We spent some time with him at the winery, and I learned that he graduated from the University of Texas and initially worked with Kendall-Jackson..

We tasted through most of the lineup of Arista Wines, which were all dynamite. At the end, when I started talking about Zinfandel, he opened a bottle of Mauritson Zinfandel made by Mark's friend, Clay Mauritson. Clay is the sixth generation of grape growers in the family—Mauritson Winery is an excellent stop in Dry Creek Valley as I visited them myself later in my month's visit based on that experience with Mark at Arista.

The grounds at Arista Winery are beautiful, with rolling hills and captivating foliage. The architecture is Asian-inspired, with well-kept Japanese gardens surrounding the tasting room. Matt Courtney is a talented winemaker who previously spent eight years with Helen Turley, and he also has a delicious wine that he produces, Ferren.

On another occasion, we spoke with Mark at the "Healdsburg Crush" event in the Plaza in Healdsburg. The crowd around his table told you that I wasn't the only one who recognized how super the Arista wines are.

Arista is not a big production winery, so it's not easy to secure—but it's worth seeking out. They have several single vineyard wines. The Russian River Valley Pinot Noir (cuvee of several vineyards) is entry-level, and I find it an excellent pinot.

I like their chardonnays a lot (try Ritchie Vineyard), but if I had to pick a single vineyard pinot from their lineup, I might go with the Kanzler Vineyard. This vineyard is on the western edge of the Russian River Valley and is very sought after for fruit. If you find a bottle, consider yourself lucky and enjoy!

7015 Westside Road, Healdsburg .... 707-473-0606 .... www.aristawinery.com

PORTER CREEK VINEYARDS

This is as far away from Napa Valley as you can get. No glitz and glamour here. It's just as "The San Francisco Chronicle" once described Porter Creek—one of the "Homiest" wineries in Wine Country.

Although there is no pretension, the wines are tasty. The winery is located in a bend (close to McMurray Ranch) at the very southern end of the famed Westside Road. It's next to the actual Porter Creek, one of the major tributaries to the Russian River on Westside Road.

In 1978, George Davis purchased 40 acres at this site before the Russian River Valley AVA was even established. George felt the conditions at the site were perfect for Burgundian varietals, so he planted ten acres of chardonnay to go along with the existing 12 acres of pinot noir that were planted when he purchased the property.

In 1997, George turned the winemaking over to his son, Alex, who was 26 years old at the time and is still in charge today. Alex had previously worked with the renowned Marcel Guigal in France. As Alex's tenure evolved, he transitioned the vineyards to Biodynamic Farming. Porter Creek is also Certified Organic.

I like the entry-level Porter Creek Pinot Noir Russian River Valley, but be forewarned that this pinot noir is a little more reserved in style than many Russian River pinots. The bottling worth seeking (if you can find it—hardly any Porter Creek in distribution) is the Porter Creek Hillside Old Vine Pinot Noir. Pretty serious pinot!

I also enjoy a few varietals from Porter Creek that you don't see much of in Sonoma. One good with pizza or spaghetti is the Porter Creek "Old Vine" Carignane (from a vineyard planted in 1939 in Mendocino). Carignane is a grape (sometimes used as a blending grape with other varietals) that was widely grown in the late 1800s to the mid-1900s in California.

The other unique varietal that you find a little more of in Sonoma (but certainly not a lot of it—perhaps 240 acres in all of Sonoma County) is the Porter Creek Viognier Hayley Marie Vineyard. Porter Creek has been making viognier for 20 years but only recently started making it from their estate vineyards. A lovely summer wine!

8735 Westside Road, Healdsburg .... 707-433-6321 .... www.portercreekvineyards.com

J ROCHIOLI VINEYARDS AND WINERY

One of the most well-known and well-respected wineries in all of Sonoma Wine Country is Rochioli Vineyards. The family legacy in Sonoma began in 1911 when Joe Rochioli, Sr immigrated with his parents to America.

The family made their way to Northern California, and by the age of ten, Joe Sr. was working the vineyards (specifically Wohler Ranch) in the Russian River Valley. In 1934, Joe Jr. was born, and the family moved to a 125-acre property known as Fenton Acres.

By the mid-1950s, the family had raised enough money to purchase the property (the current site of Rochioli Vineyards). Back then, a variety of crops was planted on the property, such as beans, hops, and prunes. Joe Jr. began his work career by picking prunes at age seven.

In 1959, the family planted sauvignon blanc and cabernet sauvignon grapes on the property, but the cabernet grapes didn't do well, and those were eventually removed. The sauvignon blanc is still planted, and these are some of the oldest sauvignon blanc vines in California. Rochioli ranks at the top of sauvignon blancs in America.

Joe Jr. first planted pinot noir grapes in 1968 and then, shortly after that, added chardonnay grapes to the vineyard. In 1982, a small

amount of the first Rochioli wine was made by the assistant winemaker of Williams Selyem—Gary Farrell. A winery was built on the property in 1985, and the 1985 Rochioli Estate Pinot Noir was promptly named by "The Wine Spectator" as "The Best Pinot Noir in America."

Although all the fruit for Rochioli wines comes from their extensive Rochioli Vineyard, the vineyard is divided into Blocks—such as West End, East End, etc. Therefore, Rochioli has "single vineyard" (blocks in this case) wines within their estate vineyard, and these single vineyard (blocks) wines will have "J Rochioli" on the bottle. In contrast, the wines that are made from blends of the blocks will just be labelled "Rochioli" on the bottle.

The winery on Westside Road is a must-stop (make an appointment) for any visit to wine country. The vineyards wrap around the tasting room and make for an excellent setting. The estate wines (depending on availability) are poured in the tasting room.

The single vineyard wines are only available if you sign up for "The List." Once you get on The List (currently on a wait), you are offered wine three times a year, including in the fall when their highly sought-after pinot noirs are offered. The pinots are excellent, but if you can only get the estate pinot noir—you'll be happy upon consumption!

6192 Westside Road, Healdsburg .... 707-433-2305 .... www.rochioliwinery.com

BACIGALUPI VINEYARDS AND WINERY

Bacigalupi Winery, specializing in pinot noir, is one of my favorite places on the infamous Westside Road outside Healdsburg. Bacigalupi has managed to stay under the radar, as they make a small amount of wine sold almost exclusively through their mailing list.

They became world-famous to those in the know when winemaker Mike Grgich's 1973 Chardonnay from Chateau Montelena (in Napa) won the top chardonnay at the legendary 1976 "Judgement of Paris" competition over many of the top Grand Crus of Burgundy.

A little-known fact is that 40% of the grapes in that particular wine came from Sonoma County—and, more particularly, from Bacigalupi Vineyards. That 1973 bottle was shown to me empty, so don't let the bit of red wine in the glass next to it confuse you.

Charles (a local dentist in Healdsburg) and Helen (a pharmacist) Bacigalupi both had an interest in farming, so in 1956, they bought (for about $30K) a 121-acre site on Westside Road. In addition to lots of fruit trees (apricots, prunes, figs, and two acres of cherries), there were 16 acres of vines (zinfandel and others). Charles' friend, Paul Heck, who was with Korbel Winery, encouraged him to plant chardonnay and pinot noir.

Charles and Helen's son, John, has managed and overseen the vineyards for over 35 years. As things tend to come full circle, John married Paul Heck's (of Korbel) daughter (Pam), and the two of them are involved with other family members in running Bacigalupi today.

Pam is instrumental in working with other wineries that purchase Bacigalupi grapes. The other family members are the twin daughters of John and Pam—Nicole and Katey. Nicole worked for Silver Oak for several years, while

Katey spent time at Seghesio and Sonoma Cutrer. You can frequently find the two very personable twins at the tasting room on Westside Road.

Bacigalupi sells more grapes than they use for their wine as they make only about 2500 cases of wine for their label. The labels that buy grapes from them include well-known wineries such as Gary Farrell and Williams Selyem.

All the wines are delicious. I like their chardonnay and zinfandel, but I'm a massive fan of their Pinot Noirs and have enjoyed many bottles on special occasions (although the wines are not overly expensive). The tasting room is small and intimate, and Katie and Nicole will assuredly make any visit a fun and informative stop.

4353 Westside Road, Healdsburg .... 707-473-0115 .... www.bacigalupivineyards.com

ARNOT-ROBERTS

One of the least glammed-up tastings we enjoyed in Sonoma County was the Arnot-Roberts Winery in Healdsburg. The tasting area was just a large piece of wood stretched between two wine barrels outside the adjoining winemaking facility in an industrial area in Healdsburg. Still, the wines and down-to-earth people made up for any lack of glamour.

Arnot-Roberts was founded in 2001 by two boyhood friends, Duncan Arnot Meyers and Nathan Lee Roberts. They grew up in Napa Valley, and Nathan's family was in the cooperage business, making wine barrels for various wineries.

Nathan still makes all the barrels for the Arnot-Roberts wines. Nathan's grandmother, Margrit Biever Mondavi, wife of Robert Mondavi, was instrumental in designing the Arnot Roberts labels.

While Nathan stayed with the family cooperage business, Duncan eventually apprenticed with well-known wineries like Caymus, Groth, Acacia & Kondsgarrd. They made their first barrel of wine (old vine zinfandel) in their basement in 2001.

When we arrived, Nathan and Duncan were on lunch break at an outdoor area directly behind where we were tasting, so we chatted informally with them and their assistant winemaker (Caitlyn Quinn—knowledgeable and personable) about various subjects.

I found that at many lunches, they (brown bag) blind taste wines from all over the world. Arnot-Roberts is a very highly regarded winery in Sonoma County, and they make an array of varietals, including many that you don't often find in California, like falanghina, trousseau, ribolla gialla and gamay noir.

All the wines have minimal production (about 7500 cases total). I fell for the Sauvignon Blanc from the Yorkville Highlands (on the road to Mendocino from Healdsburg). Only ten barrels (250 cases) were made.

The other one I took home was the Trout Gulch (Santa Cruz Mountains) Chardonnay. All their white wines are fermented in stainless steel, then neutral oak barrels, and then back to tanks two weeks before bottling.

My favorite red was the Syrah—Que Syrah Vineyard. The vineyard was planted by Ehren Jordan (owner of Failla) and is the Sonoma Coast's oldest Syrah site (just outside Occidental).

The wines are restrained, as each wine is given minimal manipulation, thus emphasizing the authentic taste of the varietal and its terroir. No pomp and circumstance—just good wines, great people and an excellent place to visit!

33 Healdsburg Ave, Healdsburg ....
707-433-2400 .... www.arontroberts.com

DAVIS FAMILY VINEYARDS

Davis Family Vineyards is a rock-solid, casual spot located directly on the Russian River in Healdsburg. DFV has outside seating that allows visitors a nice view of the famous Russian River and good people-watching (weather permitting) as folks lounge on the banks or tube down the river.

Guy Davis was first touched with the wine bug at 19 years old when he worked in a French restaurant in Seattle. Guy, along with the chef and owner, each night had a late dinner with French wines after the restaurant closed.

Guy worked his first harvest in 1989 at a small winery in Napa Valley. The hook was fully set then, and he hasn't missed a harvest since. He began taking classes at night and on the weekends at UC Davis, along with Santa Rosa Junior College. He first made wine in 1995 (250 cases of Old Vine Zinfandel), in 1996 purchased a vineyard, and in 1997, Guy (and his wife Judy) released their first Davis Family Vineyard bottling.

Guy became marketing director for Kendall Jackson in 1994, and that year, he and Judy founded the Passport Club. Their mail-order company specialized in hard-to-find, small-production wines not in distribution. In 1998, they were purchased by a national wine retailer, which allowed Guy to focus on DFV and purchase Pinot Noir and Syrah vineyards in the Russian River Valley.

The Davis' two sons, Cole (assistant winemaker) and Cooper, are often in the tasting room in Healdsburg and great sources for stories and information. DFV makes an array of wines, but the core of its collection is Pinot Noir.

In an unusual marketing approach, Davis Family has opened a tasting room in tiny but beautiful Highlands, North Carolina. I visited Guy there a few weeks before this book's publication, and he was opening bottles, pouring wines, and visiting each table.

All the wines are delicious throughout the lineup, so you can't go wrong. I find their Russian River Valley Chardonnay to be an excellent wine, and their Cuvee Luke is tasty and unique (for Sonoma County, but not for the Rhone in France) with a blend of marsanne, rousanne, and viognier.

With their emphasis on pinot noir, there are several bottlings from which to choose—Soul Patch is a favorite. Another favorite wine is a limited-production albarino (grapes sourced from Miramar Torres— another outstanding winery to visit in Sebastopol).

I am also a big fan of their olive oil—especially the basil flavor. If you are lucky enough to see some at the winery or in Highlands, you should snag a few bottles.

52 Front Street, Healdsburg .... 707-433-3858 .... www.davisfamilyvineyards.com

APERTURE CELLARS

Aperture Cellars has generated quite a buzz with its cabernet sauvignon-centric wine lineup. Rock star winemaker Jesse Katz and his father, world-renowned photographer Andy Katz, have opened a beautiful winery between Healdsburg and Windsor.

By the time Jesse was 18, he had visited 80 countries because of his father's vocation. Until Jesse was 12, his dad had done various work, including album covers for six Platinum Award Winners (Dan Fogelberg, Doobie Brothers, etc.).

But things took a turn for both father and son when Andy was commissioned by a restaurant in Boulder, Colorado (where Jesse grew up) to do some photography in Napa and Sonoma.

The family fell in love with the beauty, lifestyle, and bounty of Wine Country. Robert Mondavi saw the photos in Colorado and encouraged Andy to do a photo book on Napa and Sonoma—which he published in 1992 with a foreword from Mondavi.

After attending college in California, Jesse worked at several Napa and Sonoma wineries, with the last being Screaming Eagle in Napa, where he was working when he made his first vintage of Aperture.

The wine garnered enough attention that Jesse struck out on his own. He also makes another wine, a malbec, called Devil Proof. That wine was proclaimed the best malbec in California for five years in a row by Robert Parker. Along the way, Jesse made Forbes's famed 30 under 30 list and then Wine Spectator's 40 under 40 Tastemaker.

We're sitting outside on the terrace (just outside the stunning tasting room filled with Andy Katz photography) overlooking the estate vineyards of Aperture Cellars. We notice a head moving around just at the top of the vines a few rows over from us when, in a few minutes, Jesse Katz pops out in front of our table.

I asked him how he became a farmer instead of a photographer like his dad, and he told me that he had a vision of his dad in the vineyards with a camera in one hand and a glass of wine in the other, and he decided the wine would be more fun for him. He spends some time casually chatting with us and disappears back into the vineyards.

The starter wine was a stunning Chenin Blanc that we loved and took home, and we also pocketed the Cabernet Sauvignon—a blend of Alexander Valley vineyard sites.

12291 Old Redwood Hwy, Healdsburg .... 707-200-7891 .... www.aperture-cellars.com

BELLA VINEYARD AND WINE CAVES

From our home base in the ridiculously picturesque hamlet of Healdsburg, we go north and make our first foray into the Dry Creek Valley and Zinfandel Country. We take the aptly named Dry Creek Road to stop at the iconic Dry Creek General Store to grab some provisions for a picnic between wine visits.

Dry Creek General Store is an absolute legend in the Dry Creek Valley—open since 1881 and purchased in 2001 by Gina Gallo. It has had many lives, including stagecoach stop, barber shop, bait shop and the site of a bootlegging operation. Still, now they legally sell wine and, more importantly for us today—deliciously prepared food.

Armed with our provisions, we took Lambert Bridge Road to West Dry Creek Road and headed north to Bella Vineyards. We pull into the lavender-lined driveway and the parking lot next to a lush picnic area, the crush pads, and the wine cave.

Scott and Lynn Adams discovered the property in 1994 when a bike tour began and ended on the grounds. They already had an affinity for Ravenswood Zinfandels. When the property later came up for sale in 1997, they sold a family soybean and corn farm in Minnesota to raise money to purchase what would become Bella (which is a combination of two of their daughter's names and translates to "beautiful" in Italian).

We opted for the Drive Through the Clouds tour (one of several visiting options available at Bella). Garrett, our personable and knowledgeable guide, escorts us into and fires up the 1973 Pinzgauer six-wheel truck for a several hundred-foot climb to the top of Lily Vineyard.

Picnic tables are arranged under a shaded area for a tasting through the lineup of wines. It's exceedingly calm and peaceful up on this hill, and you can see Ferrari-Carano and Dutcher Crossing wineries in the distance below. The Adams have a second label, Ten Acre, the name originated from the ten acres of vineyards surrounding their home in the Russian River Valley.

Then, it was back down and into the 7,000-square-foot cave. By the time we had driven back down the hill, the temperature had picked up, and it felt great to be in the cave.

We especially enjoyed the Lily Vineyard and the Maple Vineyard Zinfandels, along with their surprisingly standout Late Harvest Zinfandel. I was expecting something cloyingly sweet, but it was not fortified, and paired with a peanut butter chocolate that was provided—it was delicious!

9711 West Dry Creek Rd, Healdsburg .... 707-473-9171 .... www.bellawinery.com

DUTCHER CROSSING

We were running early for an appointment at Zinfandel icon A. Rafanelli, so we backtracked from Bella Vineyards and crossed the historic Lambert Truss Bridge to Dry Creek Road. The bridge was initially built in 1915 and crosses over Dry Creek.

The bridge is named after an early settler in the area, Charles Lee Lambert, who owned the land on which the bridge was initially constructed in the 1800s and then replaced by the steel truss bridge in 1915.

The cost to build bridges in 1915 seems pretty reasonable in that the bridge was built in 18 days for $8900 by ten men. It was designated a Sonoma County landmark in 1999. True to its name, Dry Creek was dry as we drove over the bridge.

North of Dry Creek General Store, we pull into Dutcher Crossing Winery. All the staff were amiable and upbeat. Sabrina interacted with us, and she was exceedingly efficient and knowledgeable. I'd heard from others that the folks at Dutcher Crossing were some of the nicest in Sonoma—that was certainly the case for us.

It's often said that the vibe of any staff emanates from the top, and the top would be owner Debra Mathy. She purchased the property (that includes 35 acres) in 2007 and became the first single female winery owner in Sonoma County.

The vintage penny bicycle found on the label of her wines reflects one of the last gifts her dad gave her before passing away. That bicycle is also prominently displayed at the winery.

We sat in the breezeway, as there was a great breeze that day, while others opted for the picnic tables under a foliage-filled veranda. All seating looks out the rear with views in the distance of the steep Lily Vineyard at Bella Winery.

While Dutcher Crossing has a vast array of varietal offerings (maybe 30 different bottlings), we particularly liked (and purchased) the Dutcher Crossing Sauvignon Blanc Sonoma Coast and the Dutcher Crossing Alexander Valley Cooney Reserve Cabernet Sauvignon.

The Sauvignon Blanc was clean, not woody, and delicious—bring on the goat cheese and the seafood. The cabernet was very smooth, well-structured, and not noticeably tannic. I will stop (and you should too) at Journeyman Meat Company in Healdsburg and grab a steak to grill up with that Dutcher Crossing Cab tonight!

8533 Dry Creek Rd, Geyserville .... 707-431-2700 .... www.dutchercrossingwinery.com

A. RAFANELLI WINERY

No trip to the Dry Creek Valley seeking great red zinfandel would be complete without making a pilgrimage (and an appointment) to Rafanelli Winery, so we made a 3:00 p.m. reservation. We entered the gate code and climbed the hill (while in the car) up to the winery.

The winery dog, a sweet yellow lab, greeted us. We let him in the tasting room as he walked us to the door because he acted like he typically escorted folks inside on every visit. We found out that wasn't the case, and he was escorted back out—but luckily, they allowed us to stay inside.

The Rafanelli family has been farming this land for four generations. Italian immigrants Alberto and Latizia Rafanelli settled in the area more than a century ago.

Latizia's family was in the wine business in Italy. Still, in those days, there was no place available for females in the wine profession—so in 1903, at age 19, Latizia and a brother boarded a ship headed for Ellis Island in the United States.

They then traveled by rail to San Francisco. Her brother helped her get settled and made sure she had a gun, and he then returned to the family business in Italy.

Alberto had joined the Italian Navy at 17 but jumped ship at port in Norfolk, Virginia, with the idea of a better life in the United States. He made his way to San Francisco and married Latizia.

The couple went to Sonoma County to buy grapes so that Latizia could make wine at home in San Francisco. She was drawn to this area because it was much like the wine-growing area where she grew up in Italy. They moved to the Dry Creek area in 1919 and bought the property that now houses Rafanelli Winery.

The Zin was all that I remembered it to be, and although Merlot gets a bad rap, the Rafanelli Merlot is one of the best I've had. I coupled those two bottles with two bottles of Rafanelli olive oil, although I had not had the oil before. I had seen the olive trees on the grounds, knew how good the wine is, and figured I couldn't go wrong with the oil.

We went straight from the winery to the bar at Dry Creek Kitchen for an early dinner. When I commented to the bartender how great the olive oil with the bread was, he said it was Rafanelli Olive Oil!

4685 W Dry Creek Rd, Healdsburg ....
707-433-1385 .... www.arafanelliwinery.com

REEVE WINERY

Turning off Dry Creek Road, the drive (about a half mile) up to and back from, Reeve Winery is one of the most beautiful in Dry Creek Valley. Many photo opportunities exist leading up to the winery, including the two old buildings on the left as you enter.

One (tiny) building says "Peche Merle Winery," but I can attest that is not the current Peche Merle Winery, as I recently went to their tasting room in Geyserville. It's an enjoyable tasting room environment, and the wines are delicious (try the Dry Creek Viognier and the Dry Creek Sauvignon Blanc—both charming).

But this story concerns Reeve Winery and its owners, Noah and Kelly Dorrance. Noah first hit the wine scene with a splash when he started Banshee Wines with two partners.

Noah began his interest in wine while at the University of Missouri, where he secured a job at a local wine bar. After traveling to France, Italy, and Spain wine countries for a few years, he was hooked and returned in 2006 to work at Crushpad in San Francisco.

Crushpad (no longer in business) was a custom crush facility where many smaller wineries (and individuals) made their wine. Noah made his first wines there, including the initial version of Banshee.

Noah eventually left Banshee and started Reeve (named after their son) in 2015. Kelly is responsible for the layout of the grounds and interior of the tasting room, and she has done an outstanding job as we hated to leave the property.

We were the last ones to leave, but also playing into the ambience was our host, Noel, whom we felt we had known for years after about 30 minutes.

Reeve makes several wines, including a new one, a Sangiovese from Mendocino, that I enjoyed—more fruit-forward than a Chianti Classico (Sangiovese being the primary grape in Chianti). The emphasis for the fruit used in all Reeve wines is from the Far Sonoma Coast (or Mendocino Coast, as is the case for the Sangiovese).

We couldn't resist the Charles Heintz Vineyard Chardonnay nor the Rice-Spivak Pinot Noir, and with a bunch of bottles of Reeve Wine tucked away, we ever so slowly and happily made our drive out of the winery's oak tree and vine-flanked driveway.

4551 Dry Creek Rd, Healdsburg .... 707-235-6345 .... www.reevewines.com

PAPAPIETRO PERRY

Ben Papapietro met his future partner, Bruce Perry when both worked with the San Francisco Newspaper Agency (eventually bought out by the Hearst Corporation).

The two became great friends; both loved cooking and drinking wine, and they also had the DNA of both men's grandfathers having made wine in their basements. The two also began making wine (in Ben's garage) and determined that Pinot Noir was the grape to which they were most drawn.

Also employed at the San Francisco newspaper was Burt Williams, who became famous through his brand—Williams Selyem. Ben was friends with Burt, so he arranged for the aspiring winemakers to work a harvest at Williams Selyem.

At that point, both became hooked on winemaking. By the 1990s, they felt their homemade garage wine could compete in quality with commercially sold wines.

A facility was located in Sonoma County such that wine could be produced in commercial quantities. In 1998, Papapietro Perry was born with 75 cases of Russian River Valley pinot noir.

I have interacted with Ben on several occasions, and the guy has a very warm and down-to-earth personality. He's the guy you want to share a bottle of wine (or a beer) with. I ran into him in the parking lot on this visit, and we discussed what restaurant had the best duck (a dish we love with pinot noir).

The winery has a great view of vineyards and surrounding hills from its outdoor (dog-friendly) tasting area. At the same time, inside, there is a small bar with some funny tchotchkes (t-shirts, etc.—typically compliments of the humor of Bruce Perry and his wife). I always purchase something in here.

Dave Low is a very capable assistant winemaker and an owner/founder/partner of Anthill Farms Winery—one of the most respected brands in Sonoma. I've consumed many bottles and love their Peugh Mixed Blacks and Sonoma Coast Pinot Noir.

Papapietro has made a small amount of zinfandel over the years that I enjoy, but their clear focus is pinot noir (many single vineyards). Their Russian River Valley (a blend of several vineyards) bottling is a good one and their best value, but their array of single vineyard offerings is also worth seeking out. It's hard to pick a favorite, but the Peters Vineyard is an excellent choice.

4791 Dry Creek Rd, Healdsburg .... 707-433-0442 .... www.papapietro-perry.com

RIDGE VINEYARDS

Although the origin of Ridge Vineyards was in the Santa Cruz Mountains in 1962 when Ridge produced a Monte Bello Cabernet Sauvignon, the outpost in the Dry Creek Valley is your spot if you are longing for some excellent zinfandels and perhaps a taste of their famous Ridge Monte Bello Cabernet.

Ridge Vineyards is a legendary California producer that rocketed to fame when it finished fifth in the cabernet sauvignon category in the world-famous Judgement of Paris in 1976. Then, in 2006, the 30th anniversary was held with the same ten cabernet sauvignons (from the same vintage). They were blind tasted again, and this time, Ridge Monte Bello Cabernet was named the top wine.

On Lytton Springs Road, Ridge is surrounded by 115-year-old vines that can best be described as gnarly. Ridge began sourcing grapes for its Geyserville Zinfandel in 1966 and then purchased the Lytton Springs property in the Dry Creek Valley in 1991.

Ridge Geyserville holds a special place in my heart, as it was the first bottle in which a light bulb went off on my beginning admiration of red wine. There are other very well-known Ridge bottlings, such as Lytton Springs and Pagani Ranch.

All three wines fall in the same category of "field blends" (various types of grapes), with zinfandel being the predominant grape in each. At different points over the years, they had been labeled on the bottle as "zinfandel," but that no longer is the case as to be labeled a zinfandel (or any other varietal) in California, that particular grape varietal has to comprise at least 75% of the wine in the bottle.

I also particularly like the Ridge Chardonnay Estate (from the Santa Cruz Mountains), as it's made in a less heavy-handed style than many California chardonnays. You can conceivably taste or purchase this wine from the Lytton Springs location.

Ridge also makes an assortment of minimal production wines only available at the tasting room, so that's another reason to visit, as you won't see them in distribution. If you are fortunate (as I was on my last visit), they may even pour the Ridge Monte Bello Cabernet Sauvignon—so make an appointment and visit.

When I am having ribs, I typically think of Zinfandel, and I've consumed many a bottle of Ridge with them. Recently, a friend told me he had tried a Ridge Geyserville with some peppery, spicy fried chicken— and he liked it. So, I tried the fried chicken with black beans blended into a little spicy barbecue sauce, and it was tasty. Give it a try!

650 Lytton Springs Road, Healdsburg .... 707-433-7721 .... www.ridgewine.com

FERRARI-CARANO
VINEYARDS AND WINERY

Ferrari-Carano is one of the most impressive-looking wineries in all of Sonoma County. The chateau/tasting room is called Villa Fiore, and it's stunning because, aside from the beautiful Italian architecture, marble was imported from Italy, granite from Africa, mahogany from the Philippines, and lacewood from Australia. The entry and the grounds are incredibly manicured (over 10,000 tulips and daffodils bloom each spring).

The five acres of gardens surrounding Ferrari-Carano are almost as well known as the wine. You can't come to the winery without detouring off for a mesmerizing look at these beautiful gardens (2,000 species of shrubs and trees, including cork trees).

Don and Rhonda Carano (second generation Italian family) founded Ferrari-Carano in 1981. They are natives of Reno, Nevada, and Don (an attorney by trade) purchased the El Dorado Hotel and Casino in downtown Reno in 1973. Don (now passed away) and Rhonda (current CEO) developed the hotel into a premier location for fine dining and great wine lists.

In 1979, while looking for wines to place on their wine list, they fell in love with a 60-acre parcel in the Alexander Valley with grapevines.

32

Like so many before them, they began making wine in their garage, took classes at UC Davis, and fell in love with making wine.

More vineyard land was acquired over the years, and ground was broken in 1985 for what eventually would be the Ferrari-Carano winery (the first wines bearing the name were released in 1987). Don's grandmother was Amelia Ferrari, thus the name Ferrari-Carano. In 2020, the winery was sold to Foley Family Wines.

The Ferrari-Carano Fume Blanc is universally recognized; you can't go wrong ordering it, and I've ordered it countless times myself over the years. The Tre Terre Sonoma County Chardonnay is another offering that will please most palates.

Another Ferrari-Carano wine that is hard to find but worth grabbing if you stumble across is the Sky-High Ranch Pinot Noir from Mendocino Ridge. The ranch's name is worth noting as previously it was inhabited by hippies who grew another crop that also gives you a buzz. I don't know if it has anything to do with the previous inhabitants, but the wine is luscious with a finish that lingers on.

8761 Dry Creek Rd, Healdsburg .... 800-831-0381 .... www.ferrari-carano.com

JORDAN WINERY

Arguably, the most iconic cabernet sauvignon brand in Sonoma is Jordan Winery in the Alexander Valley. We arrived on a beautiful fall day around Halloween, as evidenced by the pumpkins at the entrance to Jordan.

Tom and Sally Jordan married in Colorado in 1959 and shared a great love of French wines. In the early years of their marriage, they traveled all over France like a couple of grape-obsessed explorers, and there was born the shared dream of owning a vineyard and winery in France.

One night in San Francisco, a glass of Beaulieu Vineyards Georges de Latour worked its magic and gave them the idea to make a great "Bordeaux" in California. A short time later, land was purchased in the Alexander Valley, and a 200-acre cabernet sauvignon vineyard (the primary grape of Bordeaux) was planted after tearing out the existing prunes to make room for their dreams.

The next step was deciding whether just to sell the grapes or build a winery and make the wine themselves. In Europe, many wineries overlook the vineyards below, and an ideal adjoining 1200-acre parcel (with elevation) was pursued.

The owners of that parcel had no interest in selling the property to the Jordans, but it was discovered that the family loved fly fishing in Oregon. So, the crafty Jordans bought a beautiful Oregon property with

excellent fly fishing and swapped them even for the property on which the Jordan Winery now sits. The barter system at its best!

Most of the acreage is preserved, never to be developed. However, there are about 16 hillside acres that are planted with a variety of European olive trees. The Jordans had visited Tuscany in the mid-1990s and decided to plant enough olive trees such that a Jordan Estate Extra Virgin Olive Oil might be produced—the first vintage was in 1997.

Jordan only makes two wines—their highly sought cabernet sauvignon and a Russian River Chardonnay. The Jordans initially tried making chardonnay in the Alexander Valley but soon realized the cooler Russian River Valley was a more fruitful choice.

It should be noted that the Jordan's son, John, now owns and runs the winery and has made many improvements during his tenure. John's sister, Judy, made her own dynamic mark in Sonoma County with her founding of J Vineyards in 1986, right outside of Healdsburg (J shares a driveway with the well-known Rodney Strong Winery).

Judy turned J into a real force with various bottlings, including very good pinot gris, chardonnay, and pinot noir—but her sparkling wine really popped in the marketplace. Judy sold J Vineyards to Gallo in 2015. It remains an excellent winery to visit, and its Bubble Room hosts a must-visit food and wine experience.

1474 Alexander Valley Rd, Healdsburg .... 707-431-5250 .... www.jordanwinery.com

SUTRO WINE COMPANY

Sutro Wine is an independent women-owned winery on Chalk Hill Road in the Alexander Valley outside Healdsburg. Alice Warneke Sutro is the kind of person who immediately has a calming effect on the room or the outdoors or wherever she may be.

We were running a little late to meet Alice, and additionally, not knowing exactly where I was going had left me feeling just a little uneasy, as I hate to be late for an appointment. Within two minutes of speaking with Alice, all was right with the world.

Alice's family has the 265-acre Warneke Ranch, where all her fruit is sourced. She only makes about 1,500 cases of wine, so there is a lot more fruit that is sold to other wineries (many of the wineries you would recognize, such as Decoy/Duckhorn).

The Warneke Ranch property (which has been in the family for over 100 years) is unique in many ways in that it has lots of frontage on the Russian River, includes the Mayacama and Brooks Creeks tributaries, a lake, a pond, and 80 acres of vines.

John Carl Warneke, a world-renowned architect, primarily developed the property. In 1983, he formed the Warneke Institute of Art and Architecture to host leading artists and architects worldwide. The ranch has been visited by two generations of the Kennedy family and many other prominent politicians.

Alice took us on a walking tour of the property, which was stunning in its panorama and beauty. Her very friendly and charming border collie happily hurried along in the vines, the woods, and, at times, next to us.

After the hike, we caravanned across the street to Medlock Ames to taste the three Sutro wines. Medlock Ames Winery is another excellent spot for a visit—the Bell Mountain Ranch (Organically Farmed) Immersive Sound Experience is a fun and informative outing with tasty wines.

The Sutro cabernet was very good—not tannic and very smooth. It seems I rarely buy Merlot (is Sideways still ringing in my head?), but the Sutro Merlot was excellent—so I bought some.

I've mentioned the wines in the reverse order in which they were served, and first up was the Sauvignon Blanc (only 350 cases made), which was a huge winner for us. It's aged in half stainless steel, half neutral oak and has partial malolactic fermentation. It felt good knowing I would be throwing a couple of bottles in the frig when I got home and having more to share with friends!

13301 Chalk Hill Rd, Healdsburg .... 707-509-9695 .... www.sutrowine.com

FRANCIS FORD COPPOLA WINERY

F rancis Ford Coppola's journey into wine started in 1975 with his purchase of the old Inglenook family home, along with 125 acres of vineyards, in Napa Valley. Coppola and his family were living in San Francisco, and he was coming off tremendous acclaim for his first two "Godfather" films. This success allowed him to purchase a second "country" home.

Coppola said he wanted a place where his kids could climb trees and walk in a more rural setting. He originally sold the grapes to nearby wineries, but a dinner visit to Coppola's home from Robert Mondavi changed that.

Mondavi told Coppola that his vineyards were some of the most preeminent in Napa Valley, so Francis told his wife that they would make their own wine. She pointed out that he knew nothing about making wine, and he pointed out that it wasn't that long ago that he didn't know anything about directing movies either.

Around 20 years later, he purchased the adjoining Inglenook winery and another 95 acres of vineyards. Coppola embarked on making a super-premium fine wine (Rubicon) from the estate grapes surrounding his home, but he had more financial success with his more modestly priced wines.

In 2006, Coppola purchased the old Chateau Souverain Winery outside Geyserville. He formally opened the property in 2010 with a bit of a Disney/museum kind of feel to the property (some periodicals dubbed it a "Wine Wonderland").

It's a very family-friendly property. There are 3500 square feet of heated pools and a particularly outstanding restaurant, Rustic, on the beautiful grounds of the winery. It has views (especially when dining outside) that are as good as any in Sonoma Wine Country—a restaurant you should experience! We were delighted with our lunch there.

Some of the more fascinating movie memorabilia to see at the winery are Don Corleone's desk from "The Godfather," costumes from "Bram Stoker's Dracula," an actual 1948 Tucker automobile from the movie "Tucker: A Man and His Dreams" and much more.

The Coppola Viognier was lovely and had striking artwork. Try Archimedes, a cabernet sauvignon featuring nearby Alexander Valley fruit. Another good wine, a robust red blend with a striking label, is Pitagora. Pair it with food that packs a punch—like Spaghetti with Garlic and Calabrian Chili (we had it at Rustic and loved the combo).

300 Via Archimedes, Geyserville .... 707-857-1471 .... www.francisfordcoppolawinery.com

DRY CREEK KITCHEN

The restaurant that put Healdsburg on the map as a national fine dining destination is undoubtedly Chef Charlie Palmer's Dry Creek Kitchen.

Chef Palmer had already gained massive acclaim at his New York restaurant, Aureole, which began operations in 1988. He opened other restaurants, including Aureole Las Vegas, before opening Dry Creek Kitchen in Healdsburg in 2001.

Chef Palmer didn't initially plan to open a restaurant here. Still, he and his wife (Lisa—who owns the destination store, Lime Stone, next to the restaurant) wanted a beautiful place with an agricultural backbone and a slower pace than The City to raise their kids.

An opportunity to become a partner in the Hotel Healdsburg and its Dry Creek Kitchen, along with their love of the beauty of Sonoma Wine Country, helped make the fateful decision to bring them here, and with that—changed the way people began to look at Healdsburg for sophisticated dining.

The restaurant itself is beautiful inside and outside. The outside dining overlooks the scenic Healdsburg Plaza across the street, and the inside has a contemporary dining room with the chefs working behind glass.

40

We dropped in (not recommended), as we wanted to sit at the bar. We lucked out with two seats at the end of the bar. We enjoyed the couple next to us, and about an hour after we started conversing, we learned that both were involved in the ownership and winemaking of many local wineries.

We started with a market vegetable salad with a perfect amount of Dijon vinaigrette. One of the main courses for us was Roasted Mary's Chicken with caramelized garlic, herb butter, lemon, and wilted greens. We had a Limestone Chardonnay (unoaked) that worked well with the light but very flavorful sauce.

Next was the Spice Crusted Liberty Duck with poached pear (pears from Chef Palmer's farm), duck jus, and green olives. There are no heavy sauces at Dry Creek, and this one was subtle but loaded with flavor—delicious with Bricoleur Pinot Noir RRV.

Even though all of the above was excellent, the two desserts were as good. The chocolate peanut butter bar was divine—chocolate marquise on top of peanut butter mousse. The olive oil cake with citrus curd and blackberries melted in your mouth.

Any fine dining excursion to Sonoma Wine Country has to include Dry Creek Kitchen in Healdsburg. They haven't lost a step in over two decades!

317 Healdsburg Ave, Healdsburg .... 707-431-0330 .... www.drycreekkitchen.com

WILLI'S SEAFOOD AND RAW BAR

Mark and Terri Stark own several notable restaurants in Sonoma County. They first introduced small plates in Santa Rosa at Willi's Wine Bar in 2002 (still going strong, albeit in a different location than when it first opened—still a great restaurant to visit).

Mark is the classically trained chef (Culinary Institute in New York), while Terri has a hospitality background and runs the front of the house for all the restaurants. They met in Palo Alto, married in 1999, and moved to Sonoma County, where Terri has four generations of family.

Willi's Seafood opened in 2003, and even though it has seafood in its name, for good reason, there are many tasty non-seafood dishes. There's nice indoor seating with a bar, but we enjoyed the outside dining area that overlooks the main drag in Healdsburg.

The outdoor area has heaters for those cool evenings and then bring out fans if the weather gets a bit too warm. The outside area is dog friendly also.

We arrived for an early dinner, were promptly seated, and proceeded to have excellent service from start to finish. We started with the shrimp ceviche. It was very nicely done, but it had a little more heat than I expected, so lemon, lime, and an IPO leveled it out.

Next, a charred octopus taco with pickled hearts of palm and aji Amarillo. The aji Amarillo (a Peruvian yellow chili pepper) paste also has some heat. More lime, lemon, olive oil, and a Bob Cabral Zallah Ranch (Washington) Riesling brought the dish into focus. All Cabral (former winemaker at Williams Selyem) Wines are inviting!

The octopus was tender and had a delicious charred flavor. We had one of the best white wines of the whole month, Rochioli Sauvignon Blanc—a truly excellent wine made from some of the oldest Sauvignon Blanc vines in California.

We next had the steak skewers. We also had one of the best red wines that we had for the whole trip to pair with this dish—Anthill Farms Sonoma Coast Pinot Noir.

Anthill Farms is a partnership of three young men who met while working as cellar rats at Williams Selyem Winery on Westside Road just outside Healdsburg. They make great wines (try their Peugh Vineyard Chardonnay), but only 1,500 cases of this Pinot noir, so get on their mailing list or come to Willi's Seafood while it lasts!

403 Healdsburg Ave, Healdsburg .... 707-433-9191 .... www.starkrestaurants.com

VALETTE RESTAURANT

Dustin Valette and his brother, Aaron Garzini, opened the trendy (and for good reason) Valette Restaurant in 2015 just a block off the Healdsburg Plaza and directly across the street from Single Thread.

Earlier in his career, Dustin had worked at some very famous restaurants on the West Coast, including the famed Aqua Restaurant in San Francisco and Bouchon in Napa.

His most recent stint where he rose to fame, especially in the Sonoma/Healdsburg area, was the six years he spent as Executive Chef of the nationally acclaimed Dry Creek Kitchen, working with the renowned Charlie Palmer.

Dustin and Aaron had dreamed of opening a restaurant together a few decades before it happened. Aaron's hospitality journey had him spending a decade at one of Sonoma County's first fine dining

establishments, John Ash and Company. He also did stints at Betelnut in San Francisco and the scenic Rustic Restaurant inside the Coppola winery.

On my most recent visit, we slipped into a few seats at the bar, and Aaron was interacting with all the patrons—including us. I told him that I always say that I'll get a different appetizer than the scallops, but I never do. He tells me not to feel bad that people, locals, and visitors come to the restaurant just for the scallop dish.

So, without further ado, I ordered the Day Boat Scallops En Croute—Jack Herron's Wild Fennel Pollen, White Sturgeon Caviar, and Champagne Buerre Blanc. On paper, the dish looks interesting, but in reality, the flavors are explosive—one of the top appetizers in Sonoma Wine Country.

I paired it with Cast Sauvignon Blanc—Bucher Vineyard. Cast is a very scenic winery in the Dry Creek Valley and a fun stop on the way to (and on the other side of the road from) Ferrari-Carano. This wine is made from old vine sauvignon blanc grapes in a mix of new and used oak barrels—it worked very nicely with the excellent scallop dish.

I then made my predictable move to the Coriander Crusted Duck Breast—Liberty Farms Duck, Forbidden Rice, Apple/Hazelnut Puree, and Kumquat Agrodolce (an Italian sauce—agro means sour and dolce means sweet in Italian). Valette knows how to do duck!

The dish was so good, and I paired it with a perfect Lando Russian River Valley Pinot Noir. Sam Lando has a background in sales and marketing with well-known pinot noir brands, such as Williams Selyem and Kosta Browne, before getting the bug to make his wine. There is not much of it, but it is worth seeking out.

344 Center Street, Healdsburg .... 707-473-0946 .... www.valettehealdsburg.com

SPOONBAR RESTAURANT

Spoonbar is one of the prettiest restaurants in Wine Country and one of the most alluring when the doors swing open, exposing the bar area to Healdsburg's main street.

The H2Hotel evolved from the founding of the Hotel Healdsburg (just a block down the street) in 2001. You are greeted at the entry by the "Spoonfall" water sculpture consisting of 2,000 espresso spoons and "activated" by water trickling over them.

Hotel Healdsburg began to fill up, and guests were turned away. A decision was made to build H2Hotel, and the hotel, along with Spoonbar, debuted in 2010. The same ownership group, Piazza Hospitality, opened the Harmon House Hotel in 2018 just a few doors down (and on the top floor– The Rooftop Restaurant).

Spoonbar is known for its drinks program, and on our last visit there, we sat at the bar. It was fun to watch the bartenders put together creative and beautiful drink concoctions. The crowd was energetic, and as we sipped a Joseph Jewell Vermentino, it became apparent that night was a melting pot of folks from all over the country.

Spoonbar is known to have one of the best burgers in Wine Country, so that was one of our dishes. The truffle fries that come with the burger were outstanding. The Niman Ranch Spoonbar Burger has white cheddar, tomato marmalade, and pickles. It paired nicely with a ripe Spicy Vines Zinfandel.

We also thoroughly enjoyed the Pork Chop and "Ruffles" Frites with Fuji Apple Marmalade, Summer Cole Slaw, and Dijonnaise. Both dishes were very pinot noir friendly, so we enjoyed a Sonoma-Cutrer Russian River Valley Pinot Noir and Sonoma Coma Pinot Noir—another Russian River wine.

Sonoma Cutrer is legendary and recognized for their chardonnay, but this pinot noir was delightful. The George Wine Company produces our other pinot, the Sonoma Coma. Aside from the wine's great name, it's also delicious and the type of back story that motivated me to write this book.

George Levkoff grew up in New York City and fell in love with Pinot Noir while working as a U.S. Bond trader in Los Angeles. He interned at Williams Selyem for a few years and made his first wine (125 cases of Pinot Noir) in 2003.

Our bartender told me that George personally delivered the wine to Spoonbar. His website notes his company has one employee (George) who works in the vineyards, sorts the fruit, ferments the grapes, bottles the wine, cleans the equipment and floor, writes the letters, signs the checks, among other things".

219 Healdsburg Ave, Healdsburg .... 707-433-7222 .... www.spoonbar.com

THE ROOFTOP RESTAURANT

One of the coolest, and somewhat under the radar, restaurants in Healdsburg is The Rooftop right downtown in (or on top of) The Harmon Guest House.

The views are great, the staff is super friendly, the food is delicious, and the wine list is well-selected. There is an equal amount of outside seating to inside seating, and the views go from below you to the Healdsburg Plaza and up to Fitch Mountain.

We actually visited twice—including once for a moonrise night. Still, on this particular day, we stumbled in reasonably early on a fall afternoon, with light rain falling intermittently after a full day of wine tasting. I say stumbled because when the first thing I order is Parmesan, Garlic, Truffle fries, that is typically an indicator that I am buzzed.

As it turned out, the wine tasting continued as they had some exciting varietals from producers perhaps not as well-known (and certainly not as big) as many names that you and I often see.

We started with a Kara Marie Riesling from Sonoma Mountain—perfect and hit the spot after a day of pinot noir tasting. Kara Marie Groom is a young winemaker whose dad was a senior winemaker at Penfolds

in Australia (who oversaw, for a while, the making of their famous "Grange"), so she has had some quality at-home training.

We next ordered the Elote (street corn), tajin (powder of dried chili peppers, lime, and salt) & Cotija Cheese. It was delicious and hit the spot. We paired it with a Sonoma Coast Chardonnay from Marine Layer.

From a founder, Baron Zeigler, and winemaker, Rob Fischer, of Banshee Wines (sold to Foley Family in 2018), Marine Layer (a nod to the fog that rolls in from the Pacific along the Sonoma Coast) has an outstanding tasting room on the Plaza in Healdsburg. The wines are delicious, with a streak of delicious salinity in their white wines. Must visit!

We couldn't stop there as the crowd started filling in, and the place began to get a very happening vibe—the crowd was fun, the staff was fun, and all was right with the world. We ordered the Shrimp Ceviche Tostadas with pico de gallo, jalapeno, and onion (both pickled) on a crispy corn shell.

These were splendid. I will come back and order this dish sober or buzzed. We paired it with an excellent, clean, stainless-steel sauvignon blanc (Marble Cliffs) from Guadagni Family Wines (the family has been farming in Dry Creek since the 1800s).

227 Healdsburg Ave, Healdsburg .... 707-922-5442 .... www.harmonguesthouse.com

49

HEALDSBURG BAR AND GRILL

Sometimes, you just need a great burger, wings, some fries, a couple of beers, a place to watch the game, and maybe a place to sit outside on a sunny day or under the stars in the evening when friends and family show up with or without the dog(s). The Healdsburg Bar and Grill (HBG), just off the Plaza, checks all those boxes and more.

On my most recent visit, the place had a fun buzz as several football games were going on the televisions in the bar. I place my order, get a number, sit at the bar, order a Modello, and listen to the cheers and groans ring out from fans of teams from all over the country. I went with an Avocado Burger topped with grilled onions and creamy Hass avocado—which was, and always is, a solid choice.

I love the fries here and, most often, will get the truffle fries, but sometimes I opt for the sweet potato fries. You can't go wrong with either. I also had a tasty Oskar Blues Mama's Little Yella Pils Mountain Pilsner. Oskar Blues calls it "damn good, crushable beer…take two and call us in the morning".

Speaking of watching sports, other places to consider in Sonoma County are Ausiello's 5th Street Bar in Santa Rosa and Epicenter (my favorite) also in Santa Rosa, Beyond the Glory in Petaluma, and Murphy's Irish Pub in Sonoma.

Although HBG is generally considered bar/pub food, the pedigree of the chef/owner is of the highest level. Douglas Keane established himself and shot to fame locally in Healdsburg at Restaurant Cyrus (2004-2012) located in the Hotel Les Mars, which (at the time) was Sonoma's answer to the French Laundry (champagne cart, caviar cart, etc.).

Before that, Keane, along with his partner Nick Peyton, had opened Market Restaurant in St. Helena in Napa Valley. The two are also partners at HBG, which they purchased in 2008. Along the way, Keane participated in season five of Bravo's Top Chef Masters and won the competition. He donated his winnings (about $120K) to his local co-founded charity, Green Dog Rescue Project.

Speaking of Restaurant Cyrus, after many starts and stops over the years, it has finally risen again—this time in Geyserville. That is a much different type of dining than HBG.

But HBG checks the boxes for a sports bar, location, burgers, and an excellent (dog-friendly) outdoor patio. If you're not inside cheering on your favorite team on the multiple television sets, the patio is the place to be.

245 Healdsburg Ave, Healdsburg .... 707-433-3333 .... www.healdsburgbarandgrill.com

OAKVILLE GROCERY

I t's not a stereotypical restaurant, but I've ordered sandwiches and enjoyed them on their prime people-watching patio—plus, it's so legendary that it had to make the book!

The Oakville Grocery's story is iconic in Napa Valley, known as the oldest continually operating grocery store in California's history. This outpost in Healdsburg was established in 1997 by the legendary winery owner Joseph Phelps, who was the owner of Oakville Grocery in Napa at that time.

The Oakville Grocery story goes back to 1881 in Napa Valley. It survives and vibrantly thrives in its exact location in Oakville. That location has survived two World Wars, fires, Prohibition, the Depression, and much, much more.

Joseph Phelps had been running a construction company in Colorado when he won a bid to build the Souverain Winery (now Rutherford Hill next to Auberge du Soleil) in Napa. In 1973, Phelps bought a cattle ranch off the Silverado Trail and launched his wine brand from that location.

Phelps sold Oakville Grocery to Woodside Partners in 2003, who then sold it to Leslie Rudd in 2007. Rudd was not only a famous vintner, but he purchased Dean and Deluca in 1996 and later opened an outpost of that brand in St. Helena. Rudd passed away in 2018, and the Oakville Grocery outposts were purchased by the flamboyant visionary Jean-Charles Boisset (Boisset married Gina Gallo in 2009).

The Oakville Grocery Healdsburg has a small but wonderfully curated selection of wines, prepared foods, cheeses, pastries, olive oil, and lots more—including an array of lovely gift items with the famous rabbit logo of the Oakville Grocery.

It's an excellent spot to pick up delicious picnic supplies, but it's also a great place to dine at the outside tables on the patio that overlooks the Healdsburg Plaza.

I've been here many times in the early morning (they open at 7 a.m.), also for lunch and picnic supplies—but especially in the mornings, I can't help getting the apricot bar and the pecan bar (think pecan pie) that are behind the glass at the checkout counter. They have excellent coffee, and paired with those bars—it's a great way to start the day.

For lunch or late afternoon "snack" (they close at 5 p.m.), there are a couple of sandwiches that are hard to beat—the roast turkey (with bacon and avocado) and (my favorite) the Toasted Chicken Gruyere (bacon, balsamic onions). Pick a chardonnay from the cooler inside for the former and a pinot noir for the latter.

124 Matheson St, Healdsburg .... 707-433-3200 .... www.oakvillegrocery.com

BRAVAS BAR DE TAPAS

Bravas de Tapas is another Mark and Terri Stark restaurant (part of the Stark Reality Restaurants) located in downtown Healdsburg. I've eaten at many tapas restaurants around the country, but this is close to the top of the list.

Recognized as a Top 20 Tapas Restaurants in the "U.S. by Travel + Leisure", "The San Francisco Chronicle" has also put Bravas in the Top 100 Restaurants in the Bay Area. Its rankings are as high as my blood alcohol level today, having just left "Healdsburg Crush" (60 wineries plus food vendors pouring at the Healdsburg Plaza).

Although I love sitting outside at one of the many tree-lined tables, this particular visit was so packed with hungry, very inebriated, and incredibly festive patrons—that we were fortunate to grab seats at the outdoor bar.

I love the paella, but we get the fried eggplant chips (insane), Patatas Bravas, and Goat Cheese Toast with White Truffle Honey. The soothing dishes paired wonderfully with Hawley Viognier, Leo Steen Chenin Blanc, and the legendary Merry Edwards sauvignon blanc (one of my top three sauvignon blancs in Sonoma).

Leo Steen is very well known in Sonoma County for his Chenin Blancs. I've enjoyed them for over a decade, and they are delicious. Leo (originally from Denmark) has the looks, charisma, and delicious wines that make his tasting room in Healdsburg very popular. His last name is actually Hansen, but "Steen" is a synonym for Chenin Blanc.

The Hawley Viognier was also a superb wine with goat cheese. Hawley is run by John Hawley (along with his two sons), who has a long history of winemaking, including ten years at Clos du Bois and six years making Kendall Jackson.

We made several new friends at the bar, including a gentleman in the marijuana industry. He handed me what I thought was a dessert gummy bear, but 20 minutes after consumption, the party went into overdrive for a good while.

I became famished again, so Round 2—the Skirt Steak with Valdeon Cheese Butter and Red Onion Marmalade. The J. Cage Pinot Noir Wedding Block and the Meeker Hone #2 Syrah were ordered. Charles Meeker bought his first vineyard in the Dry Creek Valley in 1977. He established his winery in 1984—all the while living in Los Angeles. In 1990, he became head of Metro Goldwyn Meyer.

The J Cage Pinot Noir was delicious. Run by the Roger Beery family (originally from Austin), their son, Conch, is the winemaker and is assisted by renowned consultant Adam Lee of Siduri fame. J. Cage is Roger's great-grandfather and known for having built the Lamar Boulevard Bridge in downtown Austin.

420 Center Street, Healdsburg ....
707-433-7700 ....
www.starkrestaurants.com

THE NECTARY (HEALDSBURG AND SEBASTOPOL)

I f you stay a while in wine country and have enjoyed a good number of restaurants and wineries each day, there comes a day when you need a different type of restaurant—one to reset your constitution. The Nectary in Healdsburg or Sebastopol is just what the doctor ordered. This was my day after the "Healdsburg Crush," and I was dragging.

The founder of The Nectary, Gia Biaocchi, was raised in Sebastopol but, after college, moved to Hawaii, where she sharpened her vegan/raw food chef skills at the Blossoming Lotus Restaurant and later managed the Lotus Root Juice Bar and Bakery.

The Sebastopol location was the first store, and later Healdsburg was opened. The Healdsburg location is right on The Plaza and is funky, super cute, and well-done with seating inside. The fresh Healdsburg Farmer's Market was on the Plaza today/Tuesday.

There's much to choose from at The Nectary as they have wellness shots, sweet and savory treats, superfood smoothies, ferments, hot tonics and nectars, cold-pressed juices, acai and smoothie bowls, and more.

I love their smoothies, and they have some fun names for their various offerings –Wild Blue Yonder, The Pollinator, Matcha Made in Heaven, Figgy Stardust, Mojo Rising, Empowermint, and The Buzz (plus more).

On my last visit, I had The Funky Monkey—blueberries, bananas, dates, chia seeds, raw almond butter, and house-made raw activated local almond milk. It was delicious, hit the spot, and went perfectly with my healthy bars, whose recipes change based on what fresh ingredients are available.

I also used the smoothie as a chaser for my wellness shots. You can feel they are healthy for you but don't always taste the greatest, so the smoothie was a perfect foil.

I had the Hot Shot, which is cold-pressed ginger, lemon, and cayenne. The Ginger Elixir (as per the menu) aids digestion, soothes inflammation, eases joint pain, and reduces swelling—all things I needed.

To ensure I covered all the bases, I also had the Turmeric Elixir; the menu says, "…promotes healthy liver function and heart health". Just what the doctor ordered!

312 Center Street, Healdsburg …. 707-473-0677 …. www.thenectary.net

7300 Healdsburg Ave, Sebastopol …. 707-829-2697 …. www.thenectary.net

THE MATHESON

Chef Dustin Valette and partner Craig Ramsey opened the stunningly beautiful, three-story restaurant, The Matheson, in the fall of 2021. The opening was a long labor of love for Valette, whose great-grandfather, Honore Valette, owned a bakery in the 1930s in this very location across from The Plaza in downtown Healdsburg.

Having gained acclaim as the chef at Dry Creek Kitchen and further acclaim at his namesake restaurant, Valette, this crown jewel is a town and visitor gathering place and continues Dustin's career ascending trajectory.

The first floor of the restaurant has a menu that has both pre-fix and a la carte options featuring local Sonoma County fishermen, growers, and ranchers. On a recent visit, I had sliced duck with cherry and kohlrabi mousseline (I'd never had or heard of kohlrabi, but it's a vegetable with a taste similar to broccoli stems—it tasted good as a mousse).

One of the top features of the first floor is The Wine Wall, featuring 88 wines on tap. For my sliced duck (which, speaking of duck, the "Chef's Reserve Selections" has roasted half duck, which is outstanding and enough for two to share), I had two pinot noir wall selections—Williams Selyem Eastside Road Neighbors and Hirsch Bohan-Dillon.

The Mezzanine Level of the restaurant is a lovely space that expands over the kitchen and has views to the main dining room below and views across to the Healdsburg Plaza. This space is typically used for private parties, anchored by their private wine cellar, but is also used as a tasting area to showcase Valette's private-label wines.

Those wines are top-notch with very outstanding winemakers, including a Sonoma Coast Pinot Noir (winemaker Bob Cabral—formerly Williams Selyem, now Bob Cabral Wines), a Russian River Chardonnay (winemaker Tom Rochioli) and a sauvignon blanc and cabernet sauvignon—both from Napa and from winemaker Jesse Katz (Aperture).

The third floor (Roof 106) has a different, more casual menu than downstairs, with a lot of energy and atmosphere, including a great indoor/outdoor dining space overlooking Healdsburg Plaza. A 3,800-pound wood-fired Mugnaini oven is the center point of the kitchen and kicks out some delicious pizza.

I love the Pork Belly Pizza with gruyere, roasted garlic crème fraiche, red onion, lemon zest, and chopped rosemary. I saw this dish on Guy Fieri's (from Santa Rosa) "Diners, Drive-Ins, and Dives," but I'd like to think I had it before Mr. Flavortown. On this day, there was a pork belly special with an Asian preparation, so I went in that direction—also dynamite!

106 Matheson Street, Healdsburg .... 707-723-1106 .... www.thematheson.com

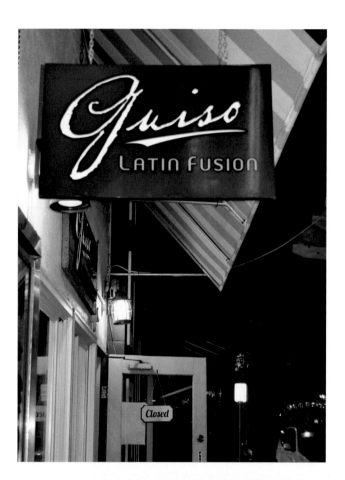

GUISO LATIN FUSION RESTAURANT

Just a couple blocks off the Plaza in Healdsburg (across the street from Vallette and Single Thread) is a tiny (with giant flavors) restaurant beloved by many—Guiso. Its authentic Salvadorian and Caribbean flavors are off the chart!

Carlos Mojica is the chef/owner, and the restaurant's success has been a family effort. The chef's mom, Margarita, makes the Pupusas, and his grandmother (Mama Yeya) is responsible for the guiso sauce that goes into several dishes.

Carlos' significant other and his sister, Valeria, have been part of several engaging waitstaff members I've enjoyed interacting with in my many dining experiences here. Sous Chef Arturo Lopez is also an integral part of the operation. Carlos opened the restaurant, along with his dad (Carlos), in 2015 when he was just 24 years old.

Carols started his career as a dishwasher at Jackson's Bar and Oven in Santa Rosa and advanced up to line cook within three years. Guiso's menu is small, which allows the chef to zone in on the few dishes that are offered.

This evening, we started with the Camarones Borrachas—Spicy wild tiger prawns, Grandma's tomato Guiso sauce, wild arugula, toasted sesame seeds, and fingerling potatoes. The dish was so explosive it should have a warning label.

We had two great wines with the dish—Bucher Sauvignon Blanc and Aldina Chardonnay. The Aldina name is an homage to the winery owners' (brother/sister, Francisco, and Monica Lopez) parents, whose names happen to be Al and Dina.

The Lopez family also owns Bacchus Landing just outside downtown Healdsburg as you head out Westside Road. It's a must-stop in Healdsburg (several wineries, including Dan Kosta's Convene Winery, pour their wines from this location).

Although the paella is phenomenal, I'm always tempted by (and got) the Asado Argentino (serves 2-3)—a one-pound Akaushi wagyu flat iron steak, black garlic, Wolf coffee rub, and Chimichurri. Phenomenal! I also got a side of fries that were excellent.

We liked the Gracianna Pinot Noir Russian River Valley with the steak, and it was smooth as silk with a typical Russian River Valley flavor profile featuring black cherry cola. Gracianna Winery is a small family-owned (the Amadors) winery whose name comes from their maternal grandmother, Gracianna Lasaga—a cool place to visit!

Guiso is tiny, but the flavors are huge. The intimacy, friendliness, professionalism of the staff, and the outstanding food, along with a small but well-thought-out wine list—make Guiso a spot that would be a culinary crime to miss on a trip to Sonoma Wine Country.

117 North Street, Healdsburg .... 707-431-1302 .... www.guisolatinfusion.com

RUSTIC RESTAURANT

My pick for the most scenic restaurant setting in which to dine in all of Sonoma Wine Country is on the patio at Rustic at the Francis Ford Coppola Winery in Geyserville.

Rustic was opened in 2010, and Francis was very hands-on related to the menu and all else that was initially put in place. In fact, there is an outlined center section of the menu called "Francis's Favorites"—a few of his favorite dishes (with accompanying comments by Francis).

We arrived for lunch on an absolutely stunning fall afternoon. We were lucky enough to secure a table at the edge of the fantastic patio (the inside of the restaurant is very cool, too, with high ceilings and good views as well). On the patio, we could almost reach out and touch the vines, and we actually could reach out and touch the roses.

Two things that can't be missed before getting to the main course are the Zucchini Fries (absolutely addictive) and the savory zeppole (fried Italian doughnuts) that are light as air and also addictive.

I felt it almost mandatory to go with one of Francis's Favorites, so I ordered the Chicken Mattone. Part of what is quoted is, "This dish, chicken under stone or brick, has become popular lately, but often too tame compared to my favorite version. You have to drive to the outskirts of Rome about 45 minutes and call ahead because this is how long it takes to prepare it authentically. I went in the kitchen and watched an old man make it".

Francis must have made good notes because my chicken was delicious—skin crispness with lively seasoning on the outside and juicy and soft on the inside. The vegetables served under the chicken seemed to have some chicken drippings flavored in—a delicious dish!

We also had spaghetti with meat sauce (excellent) paired wonderfully with a Coppola wine, Pitagoria. The wine is named after the Greek scholar Pythagoras—Pitagoria in Italian. The wine blends many varietals, including zinfandel, syrah, cabernet sauvignon, cabernet franc and malbec. It's tasty and looks great sitting on the table, too.

The staff is engaging and knowledgeable, the management team keeps things running smoothly, and Executive Chef Tim Bodell knows how to prepare and present beautiful dishes from the kitchen—an excellent place to dine!

300 Via Archemides, Geyserville .... 707-857-1445 .... www.francisfordcoppolawinery.com

THE MONTAGE RESORT RESTAURANTS

The Montage Resort right outside Healdsburg is a beautiful, very high-end property that houses three restaurants—Hudson Springs Bar and Grill, a casual eatery by the pool that is open seasonally, Scout Field Bar in the center of the lobby with stunning views, and Hazel Hill, which is the attractive main dining hall with equally stunning views.

The Montage property (117 acres) is tucked away and up a hill, so you can't see it from the main road (Healdsburg Avenue). The drive up is highly scenic, with plenty of oak trees and vineyards leading up to the entry of the property, which contains 130 rooms (not inexpensive and each one stunning) and an 11,500 square foot spa.

The 16 acres of vineyards are managed by young superstar winemaker Jesse Katz, who owns Aperture on the other end of Healdsburg. The plan is for Jesse to make wines from the grapes on the property that will only be sold at the property.

Although Hazel Hill is the main restaurant and the place to settle in for a beautiful meal—I enjoy the Scout Field Bar, with its glass-enclosed fireplace overlooking beautiful vineyards, enjoyed from the bar, couches, or outside on the terrace.

On my most recent visit, I slid up to the small bar (only about eight seats) at the Scout Field Bar and enjoyed a lovely Sunday lunch. Although I was there during the day on this occasion, on certain evenings, live music is played.

I started by noshing on some olives and toasted almonds while I tried a couple of white wines from the tiny but very well-selected wines-by-the-glass offerings. I started with an Arbe Garbe (which means "bad weeds") White Blend Sonoma Valley. Any type of wine from this producer sells out quickly, so it's worth a purchase if you see a bottle.

The second white was Senses Chardonnay, Charles Heintz Vineyard, Sonoma Coast. It knocked my socks off. The three young founders grew up just outside of Occidental and collaborate with famed winemaker Thomas Rivers Brown to make excellent wines all across their portfolio (mostly chardonnay and pinot noir). Look for their wines!

I got, and loved, the Steak Frites with charred onion and au poivre sauce. I had a Gamay Noir (the grape used in Beaujolais but rarely seen in America) from Gros Ventre, and a Small Vines Russian River Valley pinot noir—both outstanding!

The last glass of the day—The Setting Cabernet Sauvignon Alexander Valley. It is a collaboration between Jesse Katz, Noah McMahon, and Jeff Cova. A 2019 six-liter bottling of The Setting Cabernet sold for $1 million at a charity wine auction. It seemed cheap at $28 per glass in light of the $1 million—get it with the steak and live a little!

100 Montage Way, Healdsburg .... 707-979-9000 .... www.montage.com

DIAVOLA PIZZERIA AND SALUMERIA

It's hard to believe that Geyserville, with a population of about 750, has two excellent restaurants on the same tiny street—Catelli's and Diavolo. Throw in the Geyserville Gun Club (a great bar with great food) between the two, and you might even consider becoming a local fixture on the block.

Diavola was founded in 2008 by Dino Bugica. Bugica was the chef at Santi (which is where Catelli's, a few doors down, is now located) when he decided to open a new pizzeria, Diavolo (which means "she-devil" in Italian).

Back then, Santi had established itself for high-end Italian food. Bugica wanted to branch out to a more uncomplicated Italian cuisine with pizza, antipasti, sandwiches, etc.—and he did just that with Diavola.

On my most recent visit to Diavola, of course, I went with the pizza—in this case, the Sonja. It features tomato, thinly sliced onions, garlic, mascarpone, prosciutto, and Arugula. The crust was smoky and charred, the mascarpone creamy, the prosciutto salty and porky, and the Arugula peppery and crunchy. All in all—it's a great combination.

We also got the Gnocchi with Red Shrimp—wild mushrooms, basil, Meyer lemon, leeks, chives, asparagus brown butter, porcini crema, and pecorino. This is decadent and screams out for chardonnay and also screams out for some bread to offset the richness of the dish.

I was hungover (my semi-frequent companion while writing this book) on this particular day. To get back in the swing of things, we started with red and white wine for the dishes. However, we quickly switched to ice-cold beer as that was all the hair of the dog that we needed, and it worked great with the food.

Although the desserts are not wildly complicated in the preparation, they are expertly done. I loved two desserts on this occasion—the ricotta cheesecake with pears and toasted pecans and the Cannoli with ricotta and mascarpone with dark chocolate and citrus marmalade.

It's a plus that they have a television over the bar, as taking in a football game on a fall afternoon with a beverage and delicious pizza in front of you is a very comforting thing.

21021 Geyserville Ave, Geyserville .... 707-814-0111 .... www.diavolapizzeria.com

CYRUS RESTAURANT

After seven successful years (and a couple of Michelin Stars), Cyrus Restaurant closed its doors in downtown Healdsburg in 2012. A landlord kerfuffle triggered the closure, and most observers expected to see Chef/Owner Douglas Keane and long-time business partner Nick Peyton resurface again reasonably quickly in a new location.

There were several stops and starts along the way. Once, a new location seemed to have been secured in 2014 near the famous Jimtown Store and then in 2017 in another Alexander Valley location. Finally, a highly heralded opening in Geyserville in September 2022 marked a new era (and a new Michelin Star) for Cyrus.

The new location, a former prune packing plant, is 8,000 square feet of concrete and glass on just over an acre amid Geyserville vineyards. The stunning entry road gives you the sense something special is around the bend—and there is!

Chef Keane found time to be the winner of "Top Chef Masters" but always kept his eye on reopening Cyrus. The chef is quite visible throughout the moveable dining feast. The exceptionally smooth and amiable maître d' Peyton is most involved in the early stage of the experience—especially at our first stop in the Bubbles Lounge.

The first appetizer in that room was five different small bite canapes that reflected the five tastes. A couple of the bites on a large tray were tomato jam on top of a Parmesan tart crust, and a charred radish served on a bit of matcha butter.

After that experience, we were off to the kitchen table. Chef Keane presented each of the seven courses to follow from the U-shaped counter. The group's finale was billi bi, a mussel soup flavored with fennel—delicious!

The room was beautiful, and from our seats, we could see not only all our fellow diners (a total of 12) but the beautifully laid out kitchen with the staff busily making drinks and preparing the plates. We were invited to get up and walk through the kitchen to converse with all the staff—a unique dining experience.

We were then invited to the main dining area at sunset, with a beautiful view of the vineyards and the mountains of the Alexander Valley in the background. There were too many courses to describe without making this a novel, but one of the best was a beef course in consommé with squash and matsutake mushroom.

After dessert, we were escorted to a hidden room dramatically displaying a chocolate waterfall. The smell of melted chocolate engulfed the room, the Cyrus logo was lit into the cascading chocolate, and we were presented with beautiful boxed truffles. An incredible end to a wonderful journey of food, wine, service, and setting!

275 CA-128, Geyserville .... 707-723-5999 .... www.cyrusrestaurant.com

CATELLI'S RESTAURANT

We pulled into Catelli's in Geyserville on a sunny fall afternoon with visions of their famous 10-layer lasagna dancing in our heads. We also envisioned dining outside on their beautiful checkerboard patio, but alas—it was closed on that particular day.

We happily took a couple of seats at the bar and pondered what other dish we might get in addition to the lasagna. I immediately noticed the Chicken Picatta—chicken thighs cooked with capers, garlic, white wine butter sauce, greens and creamy polenta. I'm in.

We ordered a couple of glasses of white wine at the inception, and both were very good. The Unti Grenache Blanc and the Portalupi Arneis. The Unti family has made Mediterranean-style wines from their Dry Creek Vineyards since 1997. Tim Borges and Jane Portalupi specialize in Italian varietals and have a fun tasting room in Healdsburg.

Catelli's was originally opened around 1936 by Italian immigrants Santi and Virginia Catelli. They couldn't afford a sign, so a painter gave them (or gave them a deal on) a leftover sign that said "The Rex", which became the restaurant's original name.

A few years after their son, Richard Catelli, took over the restaurant, he changed the name to Catelli's. He ran the restaurant for about three decades. Then Catelli's vanished for many years—but his children, Domenica and Nicholas Catelli, brought Catelli's back to life in 2010.

The ten paper-thin layers of hand-made pasta, organic tomato sauce, ricotta and herb cheese filling arrive at the table with the Chicken Picatta. The pasta was incredibly light and delicate and just melted in your mouth. The Chicken Picatta was as good as any I've ever had, and I would definitely order that again as well.

We had been conversing with a couple sitting closest to us at the bar about restaurants and wineries when the lady, Sandy Comstock, indicated that they owned a winery on Dry Creek Road. So, we went by Comstock Winery on our way home and enjoyed the wine and the beautiful property—a nice place to visit in the Dry Creek Valley.

You never know who you might run into at Catelli's, as it is extremely popular with the locals and visitors alike. The food is really delicious, the interior of the restaurant is very comfortable, the beautiful back patio is an excellent place to dine (when it's open), the wine list is well selected, and almost 100% Sonoma wines, and the third-generation Catelli siblings have the restaurant operating seamlessly.

21047 Geyserville Ave, Geyserville .... 707-857-3471 .... www.mycatellis.com

SANTA ROSA/ CENTRAL COUNTY

TOWNS:

SANTA ROSA & WINDSOR

BUCHER WINES

Joe and Annemarie Bucher immigrated to the United States from Switzerland in the early 1950s. In 1958, they purchased a sizeable 360-acre ranch on Westside Road outside of Healdsburg and started their operation with 50 milking cows.

Their son, John, graduated from UC Davis in 1984 and returned to work on the family farm. John had the idea to diversify the cattle operation, so in 1997, John planted the first grapevines on the property. To this day, when driving to Bucher Vineyard, there are grapes on one side of the lane and tons of cows (around 600 of them on the property) on the other side of the lane.

At the time of his original planting, chardonnay and merlot were the predominant grapes being planted, but John decided to go with Pinot Noir. Another smart move John made was marrying his wife, Diane, who, along with their five children, run the operation.

The pinot noir vines began producing high-quality grapes, and they were sold to very high-profile wineries such as Williams Selyem, Papapietro Perry, Frank Family, Arista, and Siduri.

Speaking of Siduri, in 2011, the Buchers decided to produce their own wine, and they chose Adam Lee, who at that time was the owner/winemaker of Siduri (since sold to The Jackson Family), to help them make their first Bucher wines—a pinot noir and a chardonnay.

Adam Lee still works with the Buchers and is one of the most well-respected and fun guys in the business. He and Diana Novy co-founded Siduri in 1994 and enjoyed critical acclaim over the years before selling it to The Jackson Family in 2015.

A few months back at Guiso Restaurant in Healdsburg, I was introduced to the Bucher Sauvignon Blanc, a delightful revelation. But Bucher is known for pinot noir, and many years back, I was on the patio at Dry Creek Kitchen when the waiter suggested a Bucher pinot noir that they were offering by the glass.

I was blown away, and the very next morning, I went on a search to find Bucher. I eventually visited with Diane and John outside their home overlooking the Russian River Valley. That cemented my admiration of Bucher.

They now offer tastings by appointment at Grand Cru Custom Crush in Windsor. It's a lovely facility, and around 20 wineries make their wine there. When you taste, you usually get one of the Buchers to guide you. You won't be disappointed!

1200 American Way, Windsor .... 707-484-5162 .... www.bucher.wine

BRICOLEUR VINEYARDS

Bricoleur Vineyards was born in 2015 when Mark and Elizabeth Hansen purchased a beautiful 40-acre property southwest of Windsor. They embarked (very successfully, it turns out) in making the estate even more beautiful with plantings, remakes, and additions (like a bocce court, a dramatic remake of an old milk barn, etc.), which now make it one of the more beautiful properties to visit in Sonoma Wine Country.

Mark and Elizabeth both have roots in Sonoma County as Mark grew up in the town of Santa Rosa and Elizabeth (Beth) grew up spending summers on a ranch near Cloverdale, and her great grandfather was the winemaker at Italian Swiss Colony in Asti (Northern Sonoma County).

The two always dreamed of owning a winery in Sonoma County, and once their kids were out of school—they made their move by investing in this property that already had 21 acres of chardonnay and pinot noir in place. Those grapes were sold to well-known producers, and some of the fruit is still sold while Bricoleur ramps up its production (currently at around 10,000 cases).

The Hansens initially involved Chef Charlie Palmer (Dry Creek Kitchen in Healdsburg) as a culinary advisor for their food program offered at the property. Their food and wine experience (called "Rooted") is reason alone to make this a definite stop in Sonoma Wine Country. It currently involves six wines with six food pairings, and it is kind of outstanding!

Bricoleur has a full lineup (rose', sparkling wine, chardonnay, sauvignon blanc, cabernet sauvignon, etc.) are all quite good. I like their chardonnays, including their

Russian River Valley and another bottling that is unoaked. Still, my favorite is the Special Selection Pinot Noir, Russian River Valley—classic and tasty Russian River Pinot.

In 2017, the Hansens purchased a well-known premium property, Kick Ranch Vineyard, in the Fountaingrove AVA in the southeastern hills of Santa Rosa. Several wines are being produced from this property, including a Viognier that I find to be tasty.

Bricoleur in French means to putter about without a specific plan. The Hansens have translated that further to "Flying by The Seat of Our Pants" and, indeed, have launched a second label with that name—a tasty sparkling wine. The packaging is very appealing, and a fun bottle of wine to have sitting at your table.

The winemaker is long-time industry veteran Cary Gott (who founded Montevina at age 23 and, among other accomplishments, was head winemaker at Mumm Napa Valley). His son, Joel Gott, has also gained nationwide notoriety with his wine brand and ownership of seven Gott's Roadside Diners, including Napa and San Francisco.

7394 Starr Road, Windsor .... 707-857-5700 .... www.bricoleurvineyards.com

MARTINELLI WINERY

The Martinelli family is one of the most iconic wine families in California. Giuseppe Martinelli (19 years old) and Luisa Vellutini (16) left their small village outside Tuscany, looking for land to grow grapes and form a winery in America. They ended up in the Russian River Valley, and their family has been growing grapes since 1887.

They make some of the most delicious wines in Sonoma County, and I have enjoyed them for several decades. Their wines are unfined and unfiltered and luscious.

The familiar red (hop) barn is the landmark that you will see from the distance and the same symbol that you will see on some of their bottles and a good bit of their merchandise. There are two hop barns—one is the tasting room, and the other is the production winery.

Lee Martinelli, Sr., has farmed the highly respected estate vineyards for decades along with his two sons, George and Lee, Jr. Lee, Sr. is still involved but has pretty much turned over the reins to his two sons. They farm about a dozen vineyards in the Russian River Valley, one in the Green Valley of the Russian River Valley, and four in the deepest Sonoma Coast at the Pacific Ocean in Fort Ross/Seaview.

I cut my teeth on the Martinelli Zinfandel Jack Ass Hill. This wine has been so delicious for so long. Giuseppe planted this vineyard in the 1880s, one of the steepest vineyards in the U.S. The steepest section is a 60/65-degree slope, and only a 30-degree slope is allowed today. Another tasty zinfandel is the Martinelli Giuseppe and Luisa

When Giuseppe passed away, neither older brother wanted to farm this property, so Leno (the youngest) took it on. He dropped out of the 8th grade and farmed this vineyard from age 12 to 87. At a point, someone noted that only a jackass would be dumb enough to farm this vineyard—and thus the wine's name. Lee, Sr. (Leno's only son) farmed the property into his late 80s.

We pulled in on a beautiful fall day, and the wine staff cheerfully greeted us at the door and invited us in for a sample of their wines. I'm always drawn to all their pinot noirs, and I was poured a favorite—the Bella Vigna Pinot Noir, an excellent value with Bing cherry and raspberry flavors from Sonoma Coast fruit.

Another favorite is the Zio Tony Ranch Pinot Noir. Lee, Sr.'s uncle, was Tony Bondi (Zio means uncle in Italian). This vineyard is from Tony's home estate that Lee, Sr. began to farm after Tony passed away. Tony also bought one of the last existing hop ranches in Sonoma County, which is where the winery and tasting room now sits. This wine is very highly rated by the "experts," and I certainly agree with their assessments.

3360 River Road, Windsor .... 707-525-0570 .... www.martinelliwinery.com

PIZZALEAH—WINDSOR

After a long day of wine tasting, there is nothing better than an excellent pizza to kind of sober you up a bit. One of the very best pizza joints (well, actually the best, IMHO) in Sonoma Wine Country is PizzaLeah in Windsor.

Leah Scurto has been involved in the pizza business her whole adult life. When she was 18, she applied for a job at a tiny beach shack in Santa Cruz. She worked her way up the ranks and eventually became executive chef and helped Pizza My Heart expand to 24 locations throughout the Bay area.

I've got to admit I didn't know there was a United States Pizza Team—but there is, and Leah has been a team member seven times. She won the United States Pizza Cup in 2018 with her Mush-a-Roni Grandma Style Pan Pizza. This earned her a spot in the 2019 World Pizza Championships in Parma, Italy.

PizzaLeah is located in the same Plaza as Oliver's Market in Windsor, which is a great place to shop for kind of everything—prepared foods, wine, cheese counter, etc. Leah's place is unassuming, with a few seats inside and a few patio seats outside.

It's a great fall day, so we place our order inside and grab a table outside. There is a very brisk take-out business, as we saw probably 100 pies come out the door from about 40 to 50 people (and it was only about 5 p.m.).

We got the 12" Nico Pie (all pies come in your choice of 12" or 16") and the 12" Old Grey Beard. You can also get any of the pies on the menu as gluten-free. Those come in an 8" x 8" square pan-style pizza.

The Nico comes with Olive Oil, mozzarella, roasted garlic cloves, fresh rosemary, cracked black pepper & shaved parmesan. I added Italian sausage, and this was one of the best pizzas I've had in my life. The crust was thin and crispy, the cheese soft and gooey, the sausage sweet and spicy, and a fantastic infusion of rosemary throughout.

The Old Grey Beard contains red sauce, mozzarella, fontina, Italian sausage, Calabrian peppers, hot honey & orange zest. The sweetness of the honey and the citrusy orange flavor was more than offset by the Calabrian peppers. It attacked all the senses in one pizza. If you want your pizza with a little kick, this is your pie.

This is a fabulous place with 80s music playing in the background, and if pizza is your thing—this is your spot!

9240 Old Redwood Highway, Windsor ....
707-620-0551 .... www.pizzaleah.com

ZOFTIG EATERY AND CATERING

Matt and Sonjia Spector opened their standout breakfast and lunch spot, Zoftig Eatery, in Santa Rosa in 2018—and business has been very brisk since then. And for good reason, even though the menu is straightforward with sandwiches and bowls—most everything is made from scratch, and the flavors burst out of every dish.

The two were chefs/owners of Mattyson in Philadelphia and then JoLe in Napa Valley (Calistoga), but both restaurants were fine dining. The two were looking for a little more "down to earth" dining that gave them free hours in the evening (Zoftig is typically open Monday-Friday, 8 a.m. to 6 p.m.).

Frequently, Zoftig's bread comes from right next door at Goguette Bread. It's only open a few hours per day and four days a week from 1:30—6:00 p.m., but Goguette Bread alone is worth a trip to the area. They've recently expanded and now serve frozen custard (get the pistachio!), but the loaves of bread (all sourdough) are mind-blowing!

I love the Pain aux Olives Noir (Kalamata olives and herbs de Provence), but the Zinzinriz Chocolat Zeste d'Orange & Candied Oranges is gluten-free, and it is the bomb! You are greeted in French upon entering, and the staff is as lovely as can be. Be sure to order ahead online to make sure your favorite hasn't sold out.

Back at Zoftig, I was greeted by a charming staff, with Matt running the show that day. We discussed the porchetta sandwich and our excellent experiences at Roli-Roti at the Farmer's Market in San Francisco at the Ferry Building. Matt had his take on the Porchetta sandwich on the menu that day, so I ordered it with sweet potato fries.

I couldn't get out of there without ordering the Korean BBQ Burrito, which has become almost legendary in the area (and was featured on "Diners, Drive-Ins and Dives"). It's grass-fed ground beef, house-made kimchi, carrot, daikon, green onion, jalapeno, avocado, and brown rice—get ready for the flavor explosion (pickles on the side were also delicious).

The sweet potato fries were smashing, and what I referred to as the porchetta sandwich was actually the Philly. The Philly sandwich has porchetta, broccoli rabe, and provolone—what a sandwich. Some days, they make a porchetta banh mi—if you see it, get it!

57 Montgomery Drive, Santa Rosa .... 707-521-9554 .... www.zoftigeatery.com

BIRD AND THE BOTTLE

Located on 4th Street in Santa Rosa, Bird and The Bottle is another excellent restaurant from Mark and Terri Starks (their sixth at the time of opening). The Starks opened the space in 2015 in a building that was a Victorian home in the early 1900s.

The restaurant has about 120 seats in three different areas—including three indoor dining rooms, a large bar area (still houses the original home's fireplace), and two outdoor decks. Mark came up with the name when looking through the American Encyclopedia of Food and Drink, he saw the term "Hot Bird and a Cold Bottle."

The Starks bill the restaurant as a modern tavern featuring a menu that incorporates flavors from Asia, the American South, the East Coast, Jewish comfort food, and a variety of fresh seafood—but I see it as a very happening place to dine with great food and a nicely selected wine list.

When the weather is pleasant in the evening (which is the case for most evenings in Santa Rosa), it's fun to sit outside—but on my most recent visit, I slid into the bar and, as always, was greeted by friendly and informative staff.

This evening, I ordered some delicious items from the Appetizer Menu (called "Bird Feed" by the restaurant). First up is the Smoke Poke—Ahi Tuna, Smoke Olive Oil, Soy Cracked Almonds, and Taro Chips.

The dish had Asian flavor overtones, and the melt-in-your-mouth tuna was complimented by the crunchiness of the cracked almonds and the taro chips. I like Pinot Noir with tuna, and the Martinelli Bella Vigna was a beautiful match with the dish.

Next up for me was the barbecued octopus over a creamy slaw. The barbecue was a little more on the sweet side versus the hot side and, along with the creaminess of the slaw, worked like a charm with the Hanzell Sabella Chardonnay—a neutral oak-style chard that didn't overpower nor clash with the dish.

Historic Hanzell Vineyards has delicious wines and is a lovely winery to visit in Sonoma. Their tasting overlooks the "Ambassador Vineyard," the oldest continually producing vineyard of Pinot Noir and Chardonnay in the New World.

The Bird and The Bottle is one of my favorite restaurants in Santa Rosa. Whether you are looking for small plates or large plates and looking for either inside dining or outside dining, you'll be delighted with The Bird and The Bottle.

4ᵗʰ Street, Santa Rosa .... 707-568-4000 .... www.birdandthebottle.com

GROSSMAN'S NOSHERY AND BAR

Mark and Terri Starks always nail the genre presented in each of their restaurants. In this case, it's a New York-style delicatessen with a full restaurant, bakery, and bar. Speaking of nailing genres, try the Starks' Augie's French on 4th Street in Santa Rosa (their eighth and supposedly "final" restaurant).

Grossman's name is a nod to Terri's family and Jewish cultural background, and of course, we all love a delicious deli sandwich—so they sensed there was a market for the concept. Chef Mark creates a unique and eclectic menu by melding his Eastern Europe, Middle East, and East Coast influences into the fabric of the deli.

We pull into Santa Rosa's historic Railroad Square area on a crisp fall afternoon. There is not a lot of parking, but we found a good spot fronting a little park across from the restaurant.

We considered the bar area and inside the restaurant but opted for outside dining as even though it was cool outside—there were space heaters all around. We were tempted to start with the matzoh ball soup but opted in another direction—although a couple next to us did get it and were heaping praise upon the Jewish soul food.

There are so many fantastic items on the menu—where to start? I was craving a beer and wanted something crispy and salty for a starter. I pondered the potato leek latkes (with sour cream and applesauce) or warm pistachios with orange and pine nut dukkha but went with crispy baby artichokes with a labneh and sumac dipping sauce.

The app was extremely light, and the dipping sauce made them pop. The next decision was in the sandwich department, and I had been thinking of the pastrami Reuben before I walked in the door. Although the Weinburger Pattymelt (beef, pastrami, special sauce, caramelized onions, and gruyere on rye) tempted me, I stayed with the Reuben.

An excellent Jewish deli can be defined by many dishes (some already mentioned), but the Coleslaw is one that I typically make note of. I added sweet potato fries, and everything seemed right in the world as I indulged in the three truly delicious dishes (the pickle with the sandwiches was also excellent).

Grossman's serves breakfast, lunch, and dinner—all three menus have splendid offerings. The menu is expansive, and the portions are substantial—bring your appetite. This is a special and unique restaurant not to be missed!

308 Wilson Street, Santa Rosa .... 707-595-7707 .... www.grossmanssr.com

SEBASTOPOL/ WEST COUNTY

TOWNS:

SEBASTOPOL, GRATON,

OCCIDENTAL & FORESTVILLE

HARTFORD FAMILY WINERY

Don Hartford grew up on a strawberry farm in Massachusetts. After graduating college, Don went across the pond to teach English in Spain and then flipped the script, going back to Massachusetts to teach Spanish.

Don met Jennifer Jackson while attending law school in Santa Clara in 1979. Not long after that meeting, Jennifer's dad, Jess Jackson (also an attorney), founded a winery in Lake County that he named Kendall-Jackson.

After graduating from law school, Don worked in several places, including Tokyo, a prominent San Francisco law firm, and Jess Jackson's firm. But Don's farming roots pulled him towards the wine business, where he has been involved in all facets for many years.

Hartford Family Winery was founded in 1994 by Don and Jennifer, not far from their Russian River Valley Home, only 15 miles from the Pacific. The entry to the winery crosses a charming, old bridge before the foliage opens like a curtain to reveal a theater of vineyards and a fence-lined roadway that leads to the main show—the winery.

My morning tasting was on a charming garden patio (pizza oven being prepped to be fired up mid-day). Hartford makes very highly regarded zinfandels, pinot noirs, and chardonnays with 35 single vineyard bottlings—mainly from Sonoma County but with a splash of the Anderson Valley and Sta. Rita Hills.

The offerings are all limited production (usually under 500 cases), and it's hard to pick a favorite. Still, I did enjoy chardonnays from Fog Dance Vineyards from the Green Valley of the Russian River Valley and the Hartford Court Chardonnay Russian River Valley.

I have two Pinot Noir favorites—Velvet Sisters Vineyard in Anderson Valley and again from Green Valley, Hailey's Block. Hailey is the Hartford's daughter and, in 2020, was named President of Hartford Family Wines.

I am a big fan of Hartford Family's old vine zinfandels, but I fell in love and cheerfully left the grounds, happily cradling a bottle of their Jurassic Chenin Blanc from Sta. Rita Hills in Santa Barbara County.

There is also an extremely well-located tasting room in downtown Healdsburg across from, and on the same side of the road as, the fabulous Dry Creek Kitchen Restaurant.

8075 Martinelli Road Ext, Forestville .... 707-904-6950 .... www.hartfordwines.com

331 Healdsburg Avenue, Healdsburg .... 707-887-8031 .... www.hartfordwines.com

DUTTON-GOLDFIELD WINERY

We pull into the parking lot of Dutton-Goldfield in Sebastopol on an overcast and cool fall afternoon. The parking lot is also shared by Red Car, another spot worth checking out—I'm a fan of their Sonoma Coast Chardonnay.

But today, I am thinking of some of the reds I have enjoyed over the years from Dutton-Goldfield. I like to ease into any tasting with at least one white, and we were in luck as they had available their Devil's Gulch Vineyard (Marin County) Chardonnay—which I find positively delicious (and Chablis-like).

I love to hear the back story of all the wineries, and although I felt I knew the story of Dutton-Goldfield—I always like to hear it from the staff to see if there is something I've missed or if something new has occurred since my last visit.

Warren and Gail Dutton bought their first 35 acres in the Green Valley of the Russian River Valley in 1964 (when most people thought the area was too cold for grapes). The Dutton Ranch has grown to more than 1100 acres in the Russian River Valley.

Warren passed away in 2001, leaving his sons, Steve and Joe, to carry on. Each brother started a winery—Joe started Dutton Estate in 1994, and Steve partnered with talented winemaker Dan Goldfield to start Dutton-Goldfield in 1998.

Dan came up through the ranks by attending UC Davis and then on to work with Robert Mondavi and Schramsberg but fine-tuned his love for pinot noir and chardonnay at La Crema and then with Hartford

Family. Dan was buying fruit from the Duttons for both La Crema and Hartford Family when Warren suggested that Dan and Steve partner.

That partnership was consummated at a pizza parlor in Sebastopol with a handshake agreement (it seems easier to do a deal over marinara and mozzarella than a law office). The partnership between Steve (a fifth-generation farmer) and Dan has endured the test of time, and some outstanding wines have been made along the way.

After the excellent chardonnay, I moved on to the reds, and it's hard to pick just one to recommend. I was particularly taken with two of their pinot noirs from the Sonoma Coast— Deviate and Redwood Ridge. Both have fruit from the Putnam Vineyard near Annapolis and only six miles from the Pacific Ocean.

3100 Gravenstein Hwy North, Sebastopol ....
707-823-3887 .... www.duttongoldfield.com

DEHLINGER WINERY

One of the most intimate and rewarding visits you can make in Sonoma Wine Country is Dehlinger Winery in the Russian River Valley, just outside Sebastopol and about 13 miles from the Pacific Ocean. They only make about 7500 cases of wine, and the best way to acquire them is to get on their allocation list, which takes the vast majority of their wine.

Only a few guests are welcomed weekly (no more than six in any party) by appointment. It's an excellent place for those interested in outstanding wine from a producer who has been doing it for more than four decades in Sonoma County.

As a young man, Tom Dehlinger was a pre-med student but also worked at Hanzell Vineyards, Beringer, and Dry Creek Vineyards, and in 1975, at only 28 years old, bought a 45-acre aging Apple ranch just north of Sebastopol on which he planted 14 acres of vines (including four acres of pinot noir) and also built (with his architect brother, Dan) a small winery on the property.

Shortly after that, Tom met his wife Carole, and together, they embarked on raising their family and making and selling wine. Tom built a 900 sf, three-story, eight-sided home (known as The Octagon Home and still there) to raise their family on the property. Two daughters raised there, Carmen (customer service and sales) and Eva (winemaking and operations), are now at the forefront of the operation.

In 1975, neither the Russian River Valley nor Pinot Noir was well-known for wine in Sonoma County. The best-known region was the Dry Creek Valley, and its best-known grape was Zinfandel. For the first ten years, Dehlinger's most-produced wine was zinfandel made from purchased Sonoma hillside grapes (in 1984, all wines came from the estate).

In 2017, the family purchased an adjoining 35-acre parcel planted to chardonnay and pinot Noir, once known as Garbro Ranch. Dehlinger now produces a small amount of pinot noir and chardonnay under the Garbro Ranch label, and I, for one, really like the Garbro Rach chardonnay. It's reasonably priced, the wood is barely noticeable (aged in only 25% new oak barrels), and delicious. Buy it if you can find it.

Greg was a calm and informative host on my most recent visit to Dehlinger, and he did a great job of sharing the Dehlinger story (we also compared restaurant notes) as we walked up the hill outside the tasting area/production facility.

All the wines are outstanding, but Dehlinger makes a small amount of cabernet sauvignon, which is a real eye-opener. The Chardonnay is excellent, and the Syrah is distinctive—but the pinot noirs are my favorites and worth seeking out.

4101 Vine Hill Road, Sebastopol .... 707-823-2378 .... www.dehlingerwinery.com

IRON HORSE VINEYARDS

We were celebrating a special occasion on this sunny fall day—thus, the first thing that popped into my mind was "bubbles." So off we headed to the serene Green Valley (sub-appellation of the Russian River Valley) to the legendary Iron Horse Vineyards in Sebastopol—down a one-lane road and then up a slight elevation, and we're here.

Barry and Audrey Sterling founded this site in 1976. Barry, from Los Angeles, and Audrey, from San Francisco, met while attending college at Stanford. They married the weekend Barry graduated and passed the bar exam.

After practicing law for many years in Los Angeles, the Sterlings moved to Paris in 1967. Like many people who visit (or move to) France, the vision of growing grapes and owning a vineyard danced in their heads.

Upon returning to the U.S., the Sterlings first saw the Iron Horse site during a rainstorm. Despite the adverse conditions, a taste of wine made from some existing grapes on the site convinced them that they had found their vineyard.

Many experts told them the site was too cold for grapes, but they knew from their time in France that chardonnay and pinot noir thrive in cooler climates. It was, at that time, the westernmost vineyard site in Sonoma County.

The original 110 acres were planted by Forest Tancer (who was with Rodney Strong at the time), who later partnered with the

Sterlings to build a winery. The winery officially opened in 1979. The name Iron Horse comes from the train that stopped near the vineyard in the late 1800s.

In 1985, Sterling's daughter, Joy, joined the winery and immediately made quite a splash. She was instrumental in having President Ronald Reagan select Iron Horse Sparkling Wine for his toast with Mikhail Gorbachev at the first summit meeting in Geneva. She has been the CEO since 2006.

It's a stunning vista with the estate vineyards surrounding the tasting area and production facility. It's rustic with few chairs of any kind, so most people stand at (or lean on) high-top tables for their tasting.

I'm honestly no sommelier when it comes to sparkling wine (Iron Horse does make "still" pinot noir and chardonnay—it's good), but the Brut Rose' (mainly pinot noir with a strawberry note) caught my attention at the onset of the tasting. An impromptu survey revealed the crowd favorites—the Ocean Reserve and the Russian River Cuvee.

9786 Ross Station Rd, Sebastopol .... 707-887-1507 .... www.ironhorsevineyards.com

BOHEME CELLAR DOOR WINERY

K urt Beitler, the founder/winemaker of Boheme Winery, is one of the most personable folks that I met in Sonoma Wine Country. We met him at his small tasting room in the tiny and charming town of Occidental (14 miles to the California coast at Bodega Bay via Bohemian Highway—from which the winery gets its name).

For some reason, the power was off on that day in the small strip center where his tasting room is located, but his charisma kind of lit up the room, and his pinot noirs had some electricity of their own—so all was good on a beautiful, crisp fall afternoon.

Kurt has quite an interesting back story in that, although he grew up in Oregon, his uncle is Chuck Wagner of Caymus fame. That also made him a first cousin of Joey Wagner, the founder of Meomi, and now the winemaker for an array of brands, including Belle Glos, Elouan, Quilt, Boen, etc. I've met Joey, and he's quite the character.

Belle Glos (Lorna Belle Glos Wagner is Kurt's grandmother) Taylor Lane Vineyard is the wine where the light came on for Kurt. After growing up and attending school in Oregon, Kurt came back to California (Napa) to work with his uncle at Caymus. He was instructed to head out to the Sonoma Coast to till the ground (do vineyard management) at the Taylor Lane Vineyard.

Kurt fell in love with the area and decided to strike out alone with Boheme and his first commercial bottling was in 2004. Kurt's pinot noirs (vastly different in style than most of his cousin, Joey's, wines) come from Stuller, English Hill, and Taylor Ridge Vineyards—all three no more than five or six miles to the Pacific Ocean.

Although he makes a chardonnay and a syrah (both quite good), on this particular day, we tried the three pinot noirs while listening to some great stories about his childhood and evolution to where Boheme stands today.

I loved, and love, all three of his pinot noirs that we drank in the tasting room (and still occasionally pull from a stash of them that I keep at home)—definitely in my Top 10 pinots to drink from Sonoma.

The tasting room has minimal hours, and appointments are typically Friday-Sunday. Almost all the wine is sold through a mailing list. If you can snag an appointment to meet Kurt, you will enjoy the experience/the personality and (if like me) will love his wines.

3625 Main Street, Occidental ....
707-874-3218 .... www.bohemewines.com

UNDERWOOD BAR AND BISTRO

Underwood Bar and Bistro is one of my favorite dining spots in Sonoma Wine Country and is located in the small town of Graton (population about 1800) west of Santa Rosa and half a mile off Highway 116.

Going through Graton is one route you can take if you are headed to Occidental or Bodega Bay. I suggest you take the Graton route if you are heading to either town and stop at Underwood for an exceedingly good, not fussy, dining experience.

Mathew Greenbaum and Sally Spittle opened Underwood on December 30, 2002. The two had already opened Willow Wood Market Café (still a good dining option and open across the street since 1995). One of the original investors was Greenbaum's stepfather, the actor George Segal.

The nickel-plated bar (seemingly from the mid-1900s or even an old saloon) is where we ate on my last visit, and everyone at the bar seemed to know each other before our lunch was complete. The noise level is up, but I prefer that versus being able to hear a pin drop.

The covered outside dining area is lovely, with seats spaced out and heat lamps if it gets a little chilly—which does tend to happen at many times of the year.

The main dining room has a natural, laid-back feeling and what I would describe as a French Bistro from the 1940s vibe. The dark hardwood floor and the pendant lights give off a clubby feel and a club you are glad you can be a part of.

You wouldn't necessarily know it with a name like Underwood, but many people rave about their Thai offerings. The person next to me had the Pad Thai and loved it. At dinner, Underwood has seven or eight Thai offerings.

Many at the bar spoke highly of their French Onion Soup, and that was one of the dishes we had. It was extremely comforting and perfectly prepared. A side order that you can't miss is Goguette Bread (with either butter or extra virgin olive oil). I've raved about Goguette in Santa Rosa in this book, and it didn't disappoint at Underwood.

We next went with the salmon on a bed of perfectly cooked lentils topped with some frisée. The salmon was crispy on the outside and melted in your mouth on the inside.

I couldn't get out of there without the pomme frites, and you shouldn't either. A Dutton Goldfield Dutton Ranch Russian River Valley Pinot Noir was totally in synch with the salmon and the gruyere from the French Onion Soup—a wine to order if you see it.

9113 Graton Road, Graton .... 707-823-7023 .... www.underwoodgraton.com

THE FARMER'S WIFE

The Farmer's Wife in Sebastopol is located inside The Barlow—a 12.5-acre industrial chic shopping site with hip stores, tasting rooms, distilleries, restaurants, outdoor seating, and more.

The Barlow is undoubtedly worth a visit when in Wine Country. Be sure to drop by Region, which offers around 50 wines by the glass, has an excellent pulse on Sonoma wines, and frequently has winemakers in for special events.

Kendra Krolling founded The Farmer's Wife as sandwich stands at Farmer's Markets in Marin and Sonoma Counties. She is the wife of a farmer, Paul Krolling—the owner of Nana Mae's Organics.

Paul bought their farm in Sebastopol in 1984, and to most people's surprise, he decided to plant apples. They farm different varieties of apples, with the Gravenstein being perhaps the most well-known and highly regarded.

Kendra entered the food service market in earnest in 2010, serving soups, salads, and sandwiches at Marin Country Mart. The grilled cheese sandwiches took off, she revamped the menu and dubbed her operation "The Farmer's Wife."

For me, The Farmer's Wife is another excellent place for hangover food (the patty melt works like a charm) or a casual lunch before heading out to the wineries. On this day, I went with The Bacon Avocado Club. It's a triple-decker with honey lavender bacon, Brokaw ranch avocado, little gem lettuces, pepper relish, and a little mayo. It checked all the boxes.

We also got the Tuna Melt—albacore tuna, red onion, proper mayo, aged cheddar, chimichurri, avocado lime salsa verde, pepper relish, and spicy pickles. The bread on both sandwiches was excellent, and the tuna kind of melted in the mouth.

The Farmer's Wife in The Barlow is a great place for sandwiches and also has excellent fries—an array of options on fries (can't go wrong with the truffle fries). It's located next door to The Nectary, another worthwhile place to check out (especially if you are health food-minded). The Nectary has another excellent location across from The Plaza in downtown Healdsburg.

6760 McKinley St, Sebastopol .... 707-397-9237 .... www.thefarmerswifesonoma.com

SONOMA VALLEY

TOWNS:
SONOMA, GLENN ELLEN
& CARNEROS REGION

B.R. COHN WINERY AND OLIVE OIL COMPANY

Before moving to Sonoma County in 1956, Bruce Cohn was brought up in Chicago in a classically trained musical family that included his mom occasionally singing with Frank Sinatra.

Bruce studied broadcasting in college, becoming familiar with the San Francisco music scene via a music rehearsal studio. In 1970, he met and became the manager of a local band called Pud, who later changed their name to The Doobie Brothers.

In 1974, to give his family a quieter (and perhaps saner) lifestyle, Bruce purchased an old dairy farm near Glenn Ellen. There was an existing vineyard on the site, and he became intensely interested in growing grapes.

With the help of Charlie Wagner (Caymus), Bruce was able to successfully grow grapes for the next decade that were sold to other wineries. In 1984, Bruce decided to make it a solo act and formally launched B.R. Cohn Winery and began making his own wine.

Bruce had a knack for scouting talent, as two of his first winemakers were Helen Turley and Steve McRostie—both becoming cult winemakers as the years went by. On the day I visited, it was buzzing with lots of folks enjoying wine in the tasting room (a building once used as a stagecoach stop for Wells Fargo) and basking in the serenity of the trees and the vines.

I couldn't miss the olive trees (some planted in the 1870s), about 450 of them, swaying across eight acres, and because I've had the B.R. Cohn olive oil many times over

the years—I started my visit in the room that houses the olive oils and the vinegar.

And let's not forget the music, the soul of the place. Musical instruments abound throughout the property (including the olive oil room) as a homage to the Cohn legacy. The rear of the property, a stunning backdrop for tastings (try the Sangiacomo Chardonnay), also boasts a grand pavilion, making it a hit number for weddings.

Bruce sold the winery in 2015 to Vintage Wine Estates. The Sonoma Harvest Music Festival is a charity event held several days yearly with big-name artists performing. The event is worth scheduling your next visit to Sonoma Wine Country around.

15000 Sonoma Hwy, Glen Ellen ....
707-938-4064 .... www.brcohn.com

THE DONUM ESTATE

For the best art and wine experience in Sonoma, The Donum Estate is far and away your best bet! Don't miss this experience if you are in Sonoma Wine Country.

Allan and Mei Warburg have owned this stunning property in the Carneros region of Sonoma since 2011. Allan was born in Denmark, and while in college in Copenhagen, he learned to speak Chinese and later moved to China, where he landed a job in the trading business.

Allan and a childhood friend decided to start a fashion business in China, partnered with a Danish firm (Bestseller), and, over the years, turned the venture into a massively successful business.

After some solid success in the early years, Allan became interested in art and began to collect. As the company's success grew, Allan began collecting more serious art pieces. Also, a passion for wine (instilled by his father) began to call.

His interest in wine brought him to the Carneros Region of Sonoma and a winery owned by The Racke Group and run by Anne Moller Racke. The winery was Donum Estate (Donum meaning "gift of the land" in Latin).

Anne had initially immigrated from Germany to become a vineyard manager at Buena Vista. She now has her own label (with delicious wines) called Blue Farm. Anne stayed on at Donum for almost a decade before turning her full attention to Blue Farm.

As I pull into the driveway on the incredible grounds (about 200 acres) of Donum, the sculpture at the end of the driveway jumps out. It is named "Sanna" and was done by Jaume Plensa, a gifted Spanish sculptor.

That was the first of many stunning art pieces (more than 50 from international artists) dispersed throughout the estate. The last piece I visited was "Vertical Panorama Pavilion", designed by a forward-thinking Berlin-based design firm. In the distance is the "Love Me" mirrored steel heart sculpture by a talented UK artist, Richard Hudson.

We were met by our host outside the winery with two glasses of chardonnay in hand. I tasted four delicious Donum wines (one chardonnay and three pinot noirs) that were accompanied by four delicious small plates that matched perfectly with the wines.

The standouts were the Russian River Chardonnay (paired with house-made tofu with pickled vegetables from their garden topped with caviar—all consumed in about three bites) and the Carneros Pinot Noir (paired with beet tart, marigold flower petals from the garden, black garlic and topped with truffle powder) …decadent as hell and delicious!

24500 Ramal Road,
Sonoma ....
707-732-2200 ....
www.thedonumestate.com

EL MOLINO CENTRAL

Only about three miles from the town of Sonoma is Boyes Hot Springs. Although the town does have natural hot springs, another hot attraction is El Molino Central Restaurant for world-class regional Mexican fare located right on Highway 12.

Karen Taylor is the proprietor of El Molino Central and started the restaurant in 2010. She is the first to credit her mostly all-women, Latino immigrant crew for the restaurant's success.

Taylor established her credentials with a Mexican prepared food company, Primavera, in 1991 with a stand at the Famer's Market at the Ferry Building in San Francisco.

What separates El Molino from most restaurants is how the tamales, quesadillas, tacos, and even the chips are made from fresh masa—whereas most restaurants use powdered masa.

El Molino refers to "the mill" in Mexican towns where dry corn is soaked in an alkaline solution and hand-milled into masa. The difference in the way the masa is made at El Molino translates in a very positive way in almost every dish.

I've eaten at El Molino many times and always find it highly compelling. Even writers from the "San Francisco Chronicle" have rated El Molino as the best Mexican restaurant in the Bay Area, and it has also been named one of the Top 25 Restaurants (in all genres) in the San Francisco area.

All orders are placed at the front of the building. You give your name, and your orders are up when staff appears at the rear of the building (where the seating is), calling out your name. Although El Molino has beer and wine, we were hung over from the previous day's wine adventures and opted for Coke (Diet and Original).

The "appetizer" for us was the guacamole and chips, and it was vibrant and creamy and as good as any I've had. The extra crunchy chips mixed perfectly.

The halibut ceviche tostada with avocado with salsa de arbol (a wonderful blend of tomatillos, tomatoes, cilantro, and lime with a little kick from arbol chili pepper) was light with chunks of halibut, lots of avocado, and lots of delicious flavors.

The other dish was a little heavier (half of which went home with us) but just as explosive in flavor—Chicken Enchilada Suizas. The hot plate came out with the cheese having turned crispy around the rim of the plate. There was lots of chicken, and the dish was beautifully moist and appealing.

There are many good Mexican restaurants in Sonoma County, but don't miss this one!

11 Central Ave, Sonoma .... 707-939-1010 .... www.elmolinocentral.com

DELLA SANTINA'S TRATTORIA

I could hear Dean Martin singing "That's Amore" just in the distance as I came off Sonoma Plaza. It pulled me down the street, and I realized it was coming from a fabulous little Italian restaurant that I had dined in probably 25 years ago.

I remembered that they did meats on a rotisserie, and when I glanced at the menu at the front entrance and saw duck on the rotisserie menu—I knew I was going back to Della Santina's after an absence of more than a couple of decades.

The restaurant was established in Sonoma in 1990. The Della Santina family shares a long lineage and history in the Tuscan town of Lucca, Italy.

Rob (Roberto) greeted us at the door and seated us in a ridiculously charming Courtyard. He explained his father, Quirico Saltavore Giovanni Della Santina, migrated from Lucca in 1960, moved to North Beach in San Francisco, and became a baker.

Later, his uncle, Adolph, lured him to work in the family restaurant, Marin Joes. It was established (and still going) in 1954 and is located just north of San Francisco and over the Golden Gate. After 25 years there, the restaurant in Sonoma was established.

As it had turned a little chilly late that afternoon, our gregarious waiter, Pablo, suggested a couple of soups, including the Minestrone del Contadino. This Tuscan-style vegetable soup was full of still crunchy vegetables and hit the spot before the main course.

As an aperitif, we had the Balletto Pinot Gris from the Russian River Valley. Balletto owns the eight-acre Pinot Gris vineyard located about ten miles from the cooling influence of the Pacific Ocean. The wine is bottled in 100% neutral oak and was a significant surprise for me in just how good it was. I will find this one again.

The half Petaluma duck came with zucchini and wild rice risotto. The kitchen split the duck onto two plates—a good suggestion from Pablo as it wouldn't have fit on one plate. Although I do particularly enjoy duck with a cherry or orange sauce, this was served straight up—just a perfectly seasoned duck with no frills, and it was delicious.

Duck never fails me in pairing with Pinot Noir, and it was an excellent pairing with Head High Pinot Noir. Head High is a good pinot to seek out because it is a great value and second label for the more well-known Three Sticks Winery. The Head High fruit is sourced from some of the most renowned Pinot vineyards in Sonoma, including Durell, Wildcat, and Sangiacomo.

Della Santina is a beautiful Italian restaurant just off the Sonoma Plaza. I will be back, and it won't be 20 years between visits.

133 East Napa Street, Sonoma .... 707-935-0576 .... www.dellasantinas.com

EL DORADO HOTEL AND KITCHEN

The El Dorado Kitchen (EDK) is located inside the famed El Dorado Hotel right across from Sonoma Plaza and directly across the street from The Girl and The Fig.

It's all housed in the historic Salvador Vallejo building, built in 1843. Over the years, the building has worn many hats, including a church and a wine-making facility.

They still serve wine today, but on this particular day, I made my way in shouldering a major wine consumption hangover. I was up early looking to knock out the cobwebs, so breakfast at El Dorado Kitchen seemed like a good idea—and it turned out to be.

We went with the Ham and Gruyere Omelette with fried potatoes and arugula, along with the Duck Confit Hash (mushrooms, potatoes, onions, peppers, and poached egg). The Duck Hash hit the spot, although I usually don't have duck for breakfast—but I may start now as both dishes were excellent.

El Dorado Kitchen is open to the public (although it's an excellent choice for the folks who might be staying in one of their 27 rooms) for breakfast, lunch, and dinner.

I've dined here other than breakfast, and for an appetizer, I love to start with the ceviche with fresh corn chips. No matter what main course I get—I typically get side truffle fries and Brussels sprouts (golden raisins, parmesan, and honey mustard vinaigrette).

Two of my favorite wines served (by the glass) the last couple of times I've been are the Flanagan Viognier and the Hanzell Sebella Pinot Noir. Eric Flanagan is a very gregarious

personality, and you often can encounter him at his winery just outside Healdsburg on West Dry Creek Road—a very worthwhile place to visit!

The Flanagan Viognier is a lovely wine from a vineyard in Bennett Valley, but Eric also makes from Bennett Valley a silky, smooth merlot. Flanagan has delicious chardonnays from some of the most well-known vineyards in Sonoma County, along with quality pinot noir bottlings and an easy-drinking (mountain fruit) cabernet sauvignon.

The Hanzell Sebella Pinot Noir is a very soft pinot noir and works well with something lighter, such as salmon. Ambassador (to Italy) James Zellerbach founded Hanzell in 1953. The Ambassador combined part of his last name with his wife's first name (Hanah) to develop the winery name Hanzell.

Hanzell is a beautiful place to visit, with one stop on the Hanzell tour being one of the most jaw-dropping landscapes in Sonoma Wine Country. The wines are good, and just like El Dorado Kitchen, it is worth a visit when in Sonoma.

405 1st Street W, Sonoma .... 707-996-3030 .... www.eldoradosonoma.com

THE GIRL AND THE FIG

The Girl and The Fig is one of the most well-known restaurants in Sonoma and all of Sonoma County. It's been around for more than a quarter century as Sondra Bernstein opened the restaurant in Glenn Ellen in 1997.

The restaurant moved in 2000 to its present location on the first floor of the Sonoma Hotel and catty-corner from the Sonoma Town Square. There is a large antique bar (which is where I lucked into a seat on my most recent visit) and then a dining space that opens up into an outside dining area.

Sondra had previously worked at Viansa Winery in Sonoma County, as did John Toulze at that same time. They both left Viansa, and John helped Sondra found The Girl and The Fig as her Managing Partner and took on the role of chef de cuisine.

The place was hopping on this particular day (as it is on most days). I try not to get The Fig and Arugula Salad, but as usual, I can't help myself. Psychologically, if I'm at The Girl and The Fig, I am drawn to the Fig Salad. The figs and arugula blend with Laura Chenel Chevre, pancetta, toasted pecans, and port vinaigrette. It's delicious!

I also got The Duck Confit with farro, spring vegetables, and bacon vinaigrette. Eventually, I boxed the duck for later. I was considering a particular pinot noir at home to match—Minus Tide from Mendocino Ridge (purchased at Disco Ranch in Boonville). The bottle states, "A Liquid Expression of the Mendocino Coast"—delicious!

The wine list at the Girl and The Fig has a slight slant toward Rhone varietals, primarily those that are grown in Sonoma and perhaps Napa. Typically, you will see white wines by the glass, such as Grenache Blanc, Roussanne, Viognier, etc.

On this particular day, I had Cline Viognier (The Girl and The Fig also has their own private label Viognier). Cline is known chiefly for their zinfandels, but for a few decades when I would drive in from SFO to Napa—Cline was always my first winery stop. I got it for nostalgia, but it worked very nicely with the goat cheese.

In keeping with their Rhone grape slant, I got the Mathis Grenache Sonoma Valley. Peter Mathis worked at the iconic Ravenswood Winery for over 20 years and, in 1997, purchased a 7.5-acre tract above the town of Sonoma and, much to everyone's dismay, planted grenache. I had missed seeing soft-shell crab on the menu, so I boxed the duck and ordered the soft-shell. Delicious…

110 West Spain Street, Sonoma …. 707-938-3634 …. www.thegirlandthefig.com

ANIMO RESTAURANT

After a trip to McEvoy Ranch to secure some of their excellent olive oil, we make the seven-mile drive back into the town of Sonoma for an early reservation at one of the most hyped restaurants in Sonoma Wine Country—Animo.

Don't look for a sign announcing the restaurant—there isn't one (insider tip: it's next to a McDonald's). The building is very unassuming but kind of appealing because it looks like someone's home. There is not much parking, but I snagged a spot in the rear of the building behind an auto repair shop (which was closed at that point of the day).

Chef Joshua Smookler and his wife, Heidi He, opened the restaurant in 2022 after drawing rave reviews at their previous restaurant, Mu Ramen, in New York City. Animo comes from the Latin ex Animo, which means "of the heart, sincerely".

Chef Smookler, at one time in his career, was a sommelier and wine director. The two had always dreamed of doing something in Wine Country, and when a suitable space was found (a former taqueria) in Sonoma, they made the leap across the country.

We started our dining experience with the Tuna Puttanesca—sashimi-style bluefin tuna, tomatoes, capers, olives, and shallots. It melted in the mouth and paired well with our Flowers Sonoma Coast Pinot Noir (purchased the day before at the winery and a great winery to visit on Westside Road—delicious wines from the Sonoma Coast!).

One of the specialty dishes at Animo is the whole Turbot, flown in from Galicia, Spain, and dry-aged before being prepared (you can see the unprepared fish hanging inside a cooler). We saw it come out several times, and it looked and smelled great.

But as is my custom, I go with the whole duck (great with the Flowers pinot). All the meats are cooked over a wood fire grill (also brought in from Spain), which makes for a tremendous primal vibe in the building.

Our side dish (not to be missed) was the kimchi fried rice with pastrami (flown in from Katz's Deli in New York). It was delicious and large enough to be shared. Chef Smookler brought the whole cooked duck to show before taking it back to be sliced. It was excellent, and enough left over for a couple of duck sliders the next day.

There is just one dessert (which happens to be my favorite): cheesecake. In this case, a Basque Style Burnt Cheesecake was outstanding. The overall dining experience is excellent but not inexpensive—however, it is worth every penny. For a more casual experience, try Animo's restaurant in Kenwood—Golden Bear Station.

18976 Sonoma Hwy, Sonoma …. www.opentable.com …. animo_restaurant on Instagram

GLEN ELLEN STAR

Like Geyserville, another small Sonoma County town, Glen Ellen (population about 1250) also has significant restaurant firepower—The Glen Ellen Star.

For me, it's one of the top restaurants in Sonoma County. The restaurant was established in 2012 by Ari Weiswasser and his wife, Erin Benziger-Weiswasser.

Ari (best new chef, California, as per Food and Wine 2015) interned at fine dining restaurants in Philadelphia and New York (including Restaurant Daniel and Corton). Ari married Erin in New York in 2007, although they had met earlier as freshmen at The University of Colorado in Boulder.

The two moved west to California, and Ari landed at The French Laundry in Napa Valley. After two years at the Thomas Keller restaurant, Ari left to open Glenn Ellen Star with Erin.

The restaurant is rustic and intimate, and on our most recent visit, we sat at the bar for a great view of the open kitchen and their main cooking instrument—the wood-burning brick oven. You could easily make a meal on their excellent (and large portion) brick oven vegetables.

We had the Brussels sprouts with brown sugar bacon marmalade and the cauliflower with tahini, almonds, and sumac. The house-baked bread with kalamata olives and raisins was stupidly good.

These vegetables were dynamite, and we had the Keltom Roots (Unoaked) Chardonnay from the Russian River Valley. This was a beautiful wine, but with only 130 cases produced, it will be hard for you or me to see it again.

Then (and along with the veggies), we had the Snake River Farms American Wagyu Zabuton (that's the Japanese name—in America, it's the Denver Steak), asparagus, and miso-mustard sauce. The steak melted in your mouth.

For the steak, we had the Benziger Estate Sunny Slope Vineyard Cabernet Sauvignon from Sonoma Valley—an excellent pairing. Erin comes from Sonoma County and was born and raised amidst the grapevines of Benziger Family Winery (take their Tram Tour!), her family's establishment, located not far from the delicious Glenn Ellen Star.

13648 Arnold Drive, Glenn Ellen .... 707-343-1384 .... www.glenellenstar.com

THE COAST

THE TOWNS:
BODEGA BAY
& JENNER

OCCIDENTAL WINERY

The legendary Steve Kistler founded Kistler Winery, one of the most iconic wineries in Sonoma County, in 1978. Before starting Kistler, Steve was briefly a creative writer and then studied at UC Davis before working for a couple of years at another fabled winery, Ridge Vineyards.

At an even younger age, he was influenced by his grandfather, who was a collector of fine wine—outstanding French wine. With that backdrop and influence, Steve produced his first wine (a Dutton Ranch Chardonnay) in 1979 and, from there, became one of the top producers in the country of chardonnay and pinot noir at Kistler.

In 2008, Kistler sold his majority stake in the winery to Bill Price, owner of, among other properties, Three Sticks Winery and Durell Vineyards. The plan was for Kistler to stay on for an extended transition period, which played out at the end of 2017.

Steve had always been drawn to regions with cooler climates—Sonoma Coast, Russian River, and Sonoma Valley—as these vineyards most mimic the growing conditions of Burgundy.

Kistler had invested (in 1999) in a 100-acre property on a ridge close to the Pacific between Freestone and Bodega on which he was to eventually build Occidental Winery (at times, you can see the Pacific Ocean from the winery). In 2008, he purchased an additional 250 acres and now farms 85 acres of Pinot Noir grapes on those properties.

The place is stunningly beautiful, and everything is immaculate and well-organized. We tasted in the production facility but also went to the tasting room, which was closed for that particular day. The wines were impeccable—all in a very Burgundian style, with the SWK being my favorite.

It was the only winery in the whole month in wine country where purchasing their wine never came up—because, as I found out, they had no wine to sell. It was all spoken for.

Steve's daughter, Catherine, became the assistant winemaker in 2017. His other daughter, Elizabeth, is also part of the team. Most of the cellar crew and vineyard team have been with Kistler for over 30 years. It's a beautiful story, a beautiful winery, and beautiful, nuanced wines. If you can find some, they are sublime!

14715 Bodega Hwy, Bodega .... 707-827-1655 .... www.occidentalwines.com

GOURMET AU BAY RESTAURANT

As you travel the country, you often find restaurants with the best views sometimes don't provide an electrifying food and wine experience that parallels the view. There is no such problem with the scenic and tasty Gourmet Au Bay in Bodega Bay.

Gourmet Au Bay was initially founded in 1995 by Ken and Connie Mansfield as the only waterside wine bar and wine shop on the Sonoma Coast. Ken was a Grammy award-winning producer, former U.S. Manager of Apple Records, and the author of four books, including "The Beatles, The Bible, and Bodega Bay".

The shop was sold in 2002. Bob and Cissy Blanchard owned the place for many years and moved it from Bodega Highway to its current waterfront location on Bodega Harbor.

It was sold in 2019 to the current owner, Brian Roth, who met us outside at a podium to take our order on a typically cool and windy day in Bodega Bay (it was 90 and no wind when I left Healdsburg late morning, while it was 64 and 25 MPH wind in Bodega).

Brian selects the wines and chooses only wineries that have tiny production—his choices are spot on. There is seating outside with splendid views of Bodega Bay, but the chill and wind drove me to the nautical-themed inside area with good bay views.

The food is on point at Gourmet au Bay, and most dishes are prepared in a wood fire oven. I had the best-grilled artichoke in memory on my most recent dining experience.

The Middle Eastern artichoke hearts are rubbed with Lebanese spices (I thought it was za'atar, but Brian only said, "You are close") and a tarragon yogurt cream sauce.

I also had the Salmon on top of crispy polenta cake and sauteed cabbage with garlic and shallots. The salmon had a crisp exterior but was very tender and juicy on the interior. I loved it with the crispy polenta cake.

I missed Terrapin Creek Restaurant in Bodega Bay on this trip (only 35 seats), but it's an excellent dining experience. Liya Len and Andrew Truong have garnered rave reviews since opening in 2008, and rightly so (Pork Chop and Duck Breast are primo).

I also love, but missed, on this trip, River's End (set on a bluff where the Russian River meets the Pacific Ocean) in Jenner—the food is smashing, and one of the most beautiful spots in Sonoma County. Owner (since 1998) Bert Rangel has put together an excellent (and mostly Sonoma) wine list of about 125 bottles. Romantic and Stellar!

1412 Bay Flat Rd, Bodega Bay .... 707-875-9875 .... www.gourmetaubay.com

SPUD POINT CRAB COMPANY

This particular day seemed like another good day for a drive to the coast, so off we went again to Bodega Bay (as part of a planned trip through Graton). Formerly a sleepy fishing village, Bodega Bay became more of a tourist destination when, back in 1963, Alfred Hitchcock filmed a good part of his movie "The Birds" in Bodega Bay.

We skipped going to the site where a good bit of filming occurred—The School House on Bodega Lane. I can confirm after speaking with locals that the birds don't attack, although Bodega is known as a center for bird migration. You get a lot of chattering and squawking, making you aware that they are in the neighborhood.

Our destination, like many others before us, was Spud Point Crab Company. It's a tiny (360 square feet) spot across the street from the bay and the boats. The restaurant specializes in crabs (as the name implies) and outstanding clam chowder.

In 2004, Tony and Carol Anello built Spud Point. Tony had just retired from 37 years in fire service. He had known Carol as a child as their families camped in the same area. At 18, after not seeing her for over a decade, Tony reencountered Carol at a campground in Guernville. He was blown away, as evidenced by their engagement two weeks later.

After Tony's retirement, their idea was to establish a place where people could enjoy the beauty of Bodega Bay and also re-create a vibe from a simpler time. When Tony was growing up in San Francisco, he would gravitate to Fisherman's Wharf for seafood swimming in the waters just hours before consumption. Thus, the idea of Spud Point was born.

Carol developed the New England Clam Chowder recipe (there is a Manhattan version available as well), and she and her daughter Lisa run the ship. Providing the seafood is the job of Tony and his son Mark, and their boat is directly across the street.

We tried the crab sandwich and the seafood sandwich (a mixture of crab and shrimp). They are not large sandwiches, but when paired with the chowder, definitely enough to fill you up. It's a simple recipe in that the seafood is combined with a Louie Louie sauce, leaving you with just the flavor of the fresh seafood.

We had both the New England and the Manhattan versions. Both chowders are chock full of clams and just enough diced potato to make the chowders very rustic, and it is indeed one of the best versions I've ever had. It's outside dining only and usually a line, but worth the wait. Bring a jacket, as it's always cool in Bodega Bay!

1910 Westshore Rd, Bodega Bay .... 707-875-9472 .... www.spudpointcrabco.com

129

MENDOCINO/
ANDERSON VALLEY

TOWNS:

MENDOCINO,

BOONVILLE AND PHILO

GOLDENEYE WINERY

Although this book is about Sonoma, this particular Sunday, I allowed myself a side trip to beautiful Mendocino (in Mendocino County). We had a fun day and decided to stay in Boonville for some paella and a bottle of Handley Pinot Noir at the Boonville Hotel.

Chef Perry Hoffman (formerly of Auberge du Soleil and Domaine Chandon in Napa—also Healdsburg Shed) is the standout chef. We met his owner/uncle, Johnny Schmitt, a few years back at Campo Fino (now Molto Amici); Johnny's mom is Sally Schmitt, who owned The French Laundry in Napa before selling the operation to Thomas Keller.

Disco Ranch is another must-stop if you are in Boonville. It's a tapas bar and an excellent wine shop (lots of Anderson Valley Wines) and expertly run by Wendy Lamar.

We were craving a picnic the next day, and what better venue than a vineyard setting? Goldeneye Winery offered a picnic under an old oak tree in the vines, so we were in. I knew Goldeneye had some nice pinot noirs, so I picked up a couple of duck sliders with cherry sauce at Disco Ranch—what a pairing that was, and what a setting for a picnic!

The Goldeneye story harkens back to Napa Valley in 1976 when Dan and Margaret Duckhorn, with eight co-investors, purchased acreage near St. Helena. Their first vintage was in 1978 and consisted of 800 cases of cabernet sauvignon and 800 cases of Three Palms Merlot (Wine Spectator's 2017 Wine of the Year).

The accolades continued over the years for both Duckhorn and its second label, Decoy. Duckhorn has been named one of the Top 100 Wineries by Wine Spectator over the years. A controlling interest in the winery was sold in 2007.

The Duckhorns originally purchased the Goldeneye property in 1997 for the express purpose of making Sonoma Coast pinot noir. Goldeneye is the name of a yellow-eyed waterfowl that sometimes lives in Anderson Valley during its migratory path.

We were poured Migration Sonoma Coast Chardonnay to begin our picnic, which paired well with the provisions provided in our picnic basket. After that came two single vineyard pinot noirs—Gowan Creek Vineyard and The Narrows Vineyard.

The Narrows Vineyard is a mountain ranch only ten miles from the Mendocino Coast and thus affected by strong maritime influences—summer fog and cool daytime temperatures. The wine was well made and displayed a wild, rustic character, not unlike its location.

The Gowan Creek Vineyard surrounds the tasting room and sees a lot of coastal fog. I found this wine rich and lush, and it paired perfectly with the duck breast sliders from Disco Ranch. A fun and satisfying side trip to the wonderful Anderson Valley!

9200 CA-128, Philo .... 707-895-3202 .... www.goldeneyewinery.com

PETALUMA

With its location between San Francisco and Wine Country, Petaluma has a high bar to hit for note-worthy restaurants—and it holds its own.

Restaurants like the excellent Table Culture Provisions, The Shuckery (in the Hotel Petaluma), Ribisi, Central Market, Seared, Stockhome, and Cucina Paradiso are all noteworthy.

DELLA FATTORIA DOWNTOWN CAFÉ

Kathleen and Ed Weber founded this European-style bread bakery and café, housed in a historic downtown building. A constantly burning wood-fired oven is used to make some of the best bread and baked goods in the County and arguably the country.

143 Petaluma Blvd North, Petaluma .... 707-763-0161 .... www.dellafattoria.com

PEARL

Owners Brian Leitner and Annette Yang's daytime café features eastern Mediterranean cuisine tucked away in the Wharf District on the edge of downtown. Try the shakshuka, the cassoulet, or the messy and utterly delicious lamb burger with tzatziki.

500 1st Street, Petaluma .... 707-559-5187 .... www.pearlpetaluma.com

STREET SOCIAL

Marjorie Pier and Chef Jevon Martin's six-table 600 sf restaurant is hard to find (down a sometimes dark and narrow alley) but well worth the journey. The chef honed his cooking skills with a three-year stint at The Glenn Ellen Star, while Pier covers all the other bases. The wildly creative and eclectic menu changes weekly.

29F Petaluma Blvd North, Petaluma .... 707-774-6185 .... www.streetsocial.social

SOL FOOD

Marisol Hernandez and her husband, Victor Cielo, opened their third trendy Puerto Rican restaurant location in a spacious building in Petaluma's Theater District in 2022.

On my most recent visit, I pondered the delicious Cubano Sandwich and the pollo al horno with fried plantains but opted for my favorite, Mofongo Rellenos de Camarones.

The saucy prawns with garlic, onion, and tomato served over mashed green plantains with avocado paired beautifully with my sparkling limeade (Limonada Fresca)—an explosive dish that I could eat again and again.

151 Petaluma Blvd S Suite 129 .... 707-347-5998 .... www.solfoodrestaurant.com

TOP THREE UP-AND-COMING WINERIES

VAUGHN DUFFY WINES

Although Sara Vaughn and Matt Duffy made their first two barrels of Pinot Noir in 2009, they have kept their production extremely small over the years (and kept their day jobs), but the winery is now hitting its stride.

At 24, Matt cut his wine teeth at a winery in the Sierra Foothills before moving to San Francisco. There, he worked at a Sausalito Wine Shop and met Sara. He later interned at Siduri and spent 11 years at a custom crush facility, Vinify, gaining critical knowledge.

The 2023 North Coast Wine Challenge fully catapulted Vaughn Duffy into the limelight when their 2021 Pinot Noir Bacigalupi Vineyards won Best of the Best over 1,200 other wines from 240 wineries. They make only 1,500 cases of wine—better get some quick at their tasting room in Kenwood!

8910 Sonoma Highway, Kenwood .... 707-282-9156 .... www.vaughnduffywines.com

THOMPSON 31FIFTY WINES

Mike and Valerie Thompson founded their winery in 2013 (3150 is their address on Westside Road). Mike had done very well in the electronics manufacturing business, and their love of wine led them to purchase 6.5 acres in the Russian River Valley.

The winery's location is primo, and you knew the winery was destined for success when the legendary Ulysses Valdez agreed to do vineyard management (partly based on Thompson's propensity to work vigorously with various charities).

After the untimely passing of Valdez, the well-respected Lee Martinelli, Jr. has taken over. Patrick Sullivan (formerly with Rudd and Paul Hobbs) is the talented winemaker.

3150 Westside Road .... 707-583-1595 .... www.thompson31fifty.com

MORET-BREALYNN WINES

Moret started her work career at a teen center at UC Davis and, from there, moved to Healdsburg, where she worked the front of the house at Silver Oak's Twomey Wines, Kosta Browne, and Martinelli.

Moret then moved to Hall Wines, working closely with Katheryn Hall. She set up Virtual Happy Hours with various celebrities—one being Adam Lee of Siduri fame. Soon, she joined Adam's Clarice (Pinot Noir) wine club (I'm a member and love it!).

Adam encouraged Moret to make wine, as that was her dream, and with Adam's help, Moret made her first wine in 2020. The now-engaged duo are working on several projects, but my favorite is her Stray Cats Muscadelle.

www.moretbrealynnwines.com

TOP THREE
ICONIC SONOMA
COUNTY WINERIES

WILLIAMS SELYEM WINERY

Burt Williams and Ed Selyem tried their hand at weekend winemaking in 1979 in Forestville, then released their first commercial vintage in 1983. The first vineyard-designate wine (Rochioli Vineyards) was released in 1985.

That wine won best red wine at the 1987 California State Fair, beating out 2,100 wines. At that point, demand exceeded supply, and a waitlist ("The List") was created.

The two sold the brand in 1998, but The List remains, and to visit the winery, you must be on The List. Williams Selyem has influenced countless well-known winemakers, many of whom have worked harvests at the winery.

7227 Westside Road, Healdsburg .... 707-433-6425 .... www.williamsselyem.com

LITTORAI

Ted and Heidi Lemon founded Littorai in 1993. Ted apprenticed in Burgundy and then became head winemaker (at 25) for Domaine Guy Roulot. Calera and Chateau Woltner in Napa were also stops before settling in Sebastopol.

Lemon decided that his fruit sources would come from the Sonoma and Mendocino Coasts (Littorai in Latin roughly means Coasts). Lemon makes and has for years made stunning pinot noirs that sometimes take minor aging to show their best.

Wines to seek out (mainly sold through mailing lists and a few restaurants) are Wendling, Thieriot, The Return, and the Pivot. The Estate Tour and Tasting is fantastic!

788 Gold Ridge Road, Sebastopol .... 707-823-9586 .... www.littorai.com

KENDALL-JACKSON/ JACKSON FAMILY WINES

The impact Jess Jackson has made on the wine industry as a whole has been profound. A cop turned successful attorney in San Francisco, Jackson (along with his then-wife, Jane Kendall Jackson) purchased a farm retreat in Lake County in 1974.

After converting the 80-acre pear and walnut orchard to grapes, Jackson's efforts to make chardonnay were seemingly throttled when the wine got stuck in fermentation, resulting in a residual sweetness. He decided to sell it anyway, and the rest is history.

Jackson married Barbara Banke in 1984, and the two catapulted The Jackson Family into one of the industry's major players—now owning over 50 wine brands around the world, including La Crema, Brewer-Clifton, and Stonestreet (Jess' middle name). The Stonestreet wine is delicious, and their Mountain Excursion Tour is phenomenal!

5007 Fulton Road, Santa Rosa ....
707-769-3649 .... www.kj.com

TOP THREE
ICONIC SONOMA
RESTAURANTS

SINGLE THREAD

When I think of an iconic restaurant, I think of a restaurant that has been outstanding for one, two, three decades—but Kyle and Katina Connaughton (along with co-owner Tony Greenberg) and their Single Thread Restaurant—Farm—and Inn has become an "instant classic" since opening in 2016 in Healdsburg.

It's not just that Single Thread is the only Three Star Michelin Restaurant in Sonoma County and that the food and wine experience is superb; the Connaughtons have had a tremendously positive impact on the community with their involvement in programs like non-profit Sonoma Family Meal to make meals for those in need in the community.

Kyle and Katina were high school classmates outside Los Angeles. Kyle attended culinary school and worked locally at restaurants like Spago and Campanile.

Connaugton moved to Japan in 2003 to work at Hokaiddo. That influence (among others) has made Single Thread an actual Japanese-inspired farm-to-table restaurant. The Connaughtons have their own multi-acre farm that horticulturalist Katina (with two others) oversees—thus making for incredibly fresh ingredients.

The impact of Single Thread has spread via former employees who have opened their own places like Molto Amici, Quail and Condor, Troubadour/Le Diner and Maison (Wine Bar) Healdsburg. Try Single Thread's online wine store—excellent selections!

131 North Street, Healdsburg .... 707-723-4646 .... www.singlethreadfarms.com

DRY CREEK KITCHEN

Chef/owner Charlie Palmer set the tone for fine dining in Sonoma County in 2001 and still sets a very high bar. See the full write-up on Page 40.

JOHN ASH & CO.

Chef John Ash opened his namesake restaurant in Santa Rosa in 1980. Ash was among the first to use seasonal local herbs, meats, cheeses and produce to create a fine-dining experience—pairing it all with excellent local wines.

Ash is often called "The Father of Wine Country Cuisine." His restaurant was one of the first to offer wines-by-the-glass, blind tastings and food and wine-paired theme dinners. Many people in the wine industry have cut their teeth at John Ash, including Dan Kosta and Michael Brown (Kosta-Brown Winery).

Wine-savvy Chef Tom Schmidt now heads up the kitchen. The food, wine and vineyard view are top-notch. The bar area has one of the best Happy Hours in Sonoma County!

4330 Barnes Rd, Santa Rosa .... 707-527-7687 .... www.vintnersresort.com

MY TOP WINERY
IN SONOMA
WINE COUNTRY

ARISTA WINERY

Extremely delicious wines, beautiful grounds including Japanese gardens, knowledgeable and outgoing staff, excellent winemaker and gregarious owners make Arista Winery "My Top Winery in Sonoma Wine Country."

Their outstanding winemaker, Matt Courtney, has been with Arista since 2013. After college (UC Berkeley), Matt worked at a restaurant in Jackson Hole and was on his way to the advanced level of becoming a Master Sommelier. He had a change of heart and decided that he wanted instead to make wine—especially Pinot Noir and Chardonnay.

After graduating from UC Davis in 2005, Helen Turley and John Welaufer were looking for an assistant winemaker for their own label, Marcassin, and Matt landed that position.

Brothers Mark and Ben McWilliams run the day-to-day operations after their parents, Al (a former orthodontist) and Janis, ran the show for about a decade. Mark manages sales, marketing and grower relations. Ben oversees all estate activities.

Arista's 36-acre estate is on Westside Road in the Middle Reach of the Russian River Valley. There are ten acres of vines here—nine acres of Pinot Noir and one acre of chardonnay.

In addition to their estate wines, Arista buys grapes/makes wine from about eight vineyard sites, including the legendary Ritchie Vineyard (farmed by Kent Ritchie), Kanzler Family (eight miles from the Pacific in the Sebastopol Hills) and Lucky Well and Diablo Vineyards (farmed by the family of Ulises Valdez, who tragically passed in 2018).

Although appointments are encouraged, Arista is one of the few wineries of its stature that still welcomes walk-ins (with a maximum of six visitors in a party).

Arista only makes between 6,000 and 7,000 cases of wine per year (in fact, there is a "Waiting List" to join their mailing list/the "A-List,") so grab a bottle if you see it somewhere or visit the winery for several different, but all wonderful, tasting experiences.

See the full write-up on Page XXX.

7015 Westside Road, Healdsburg .... 707-473-0606 .... www.aristawinery.com

MY TOP RESTAURANT
IN SONOMA WINE COUNTRY

GUISO LATIN FUSION

I can never get enough of Chef Carlos Mojica's delicious cuisine at Guiso in downtown Healdsburg. It's one of the few restaurants where you get an authentic "neighborhood vibe" and memorable food at every dining experience.

I'm sure the tiny size of the restaurant's interior, along with the few tables on the outside with the sidewalk running through it all, makes it feel like you are in the middle of the neighborhood. And what a neighborhood Guiso has created!

The contribution of all Carlo's family to the recipes and the fabric of the restaurant makes it unique. Carlo's charismatic dad (Carlos) was instrumental in starting the restaurant; his mom, Margarita, makes the Pupusas, and his grandmother (Mama Yeya) is responsible for the guiso. His sister, Valeria, and his significant other, Marilyn, have looked after our table in the past, and both are phenomenal.

Every dish is absolutely explosive, the wine list is small but well-curated with almost all local wines, the wait staff are attentive, knowledgeable and friendly, and the size of the restaurant makes it one of the most intimate and romantic places to dine in Sonoma Wine Country.

The Paella Caribena is reason enough to come to Guiso. It was voted Best Paella in California by Yelp. It's a Caribbean take on paella with Linguica sausage, heirloom chicken, gulf prawns, clams, tomato garlic broth, seasonal vegetables and saffron rice. It is a beautiful presentation and delicious to consume!

Strangely enough, I dream about their sweet potato fries—Papas de Comate, sweet potato fries, Aleppo chile, spiced cotija cheese, chipotle aioli and chives. Seemingly simple but oh so good!

Pictured are:

Chef Carlos and Sous Chef Arturo Lopez.
Carlos' mom and dad with Kelly Coleman of Southern Glazer's Wine & Spirits.
The famous Paella Caribena.
Chef Carlos and my photographer, Colleen.

117 North Street, Healdsburg .... 707-431-1302 .... www.guisolatinfusion.com